The mystery that rattled the unfathomable

Other Books

I came in Blind
Poetry Simplified
Princess Aneni
Grandpa's Village Stories
Kule And Pelele

Taka's Dreams Book 1
Taka's Dreams Book 2
Taka's Dreams Book 3
Taka's Dreams Book 4

Shades of Affiliation

A Novel

S. Svikiro

This edition published by Creapac publishers.
Dirschauerstr 14
10245 Berlin

ISBN 978 3 947650 91 0
CREAPAC

Dedicated to...

A placid mind, keeper of the golden keys and a daughter of old wisdom. My late sister Angeline Svikiro.

Chapter
1

The alarm clock buzzed at 4 am. Like a lightning bolt, Vera burst out of the bathroom, trailed by long blonde hair glittering from the illuminating shades of the backlight. She strolled across the room with a silk nightie molded around a lanky curved body. Her carefully sculptured oil-painted lips, bulging round green eyes shot out, revealing the kind of beauty and elegance that only exists in photoshopped models.

The fluffy thick shaggy layer of hand-made Moroccan carpet swallowed her bare feet as she mindfully reached for the alarm button. Her Dutch husband Lester of six years lay bare naked on top of the sheets. Vera glanced and marveled at his physic and structured body. Chiseled, strong results of years of hard work as a fitness trainer. "I can feel your penetrating gorgeous eyes," a deep voice came out of the dark. She giggled, "you got me. I thought you were asleep."

"I was until I got a tickle from my private silent alarm." She paused, "how come I didn't feel that magic tickle. I was next to you the whole night."

" I better hurry then," and he jumped out of bed.

"Too late got a full schedule, save it for later."

"We could reschedule, I got a full sac to of load."

He spun around and sniffed her hair. "Your perfume goes to my soul," he whispered, guiding her hand towards his shaft. She slapped it away, and he

playfully growled, "it won't take long," he hushed. "I got a flight to catch. I don't wanna be glowing on the plane." She yelled as she headed for the bathroom with him chasing after her, protesting, and begging.
"I just want a tater tot, a nimble," he stammered. She burst out laughing. Before she could shut the door, he budged in.
"I had a terrible dream last night, wifey."
"Really, oh no! What happened this time? You got ran over by a train."
He wrapped his arms around her and pulled her closer, scenting her neck.
"I dreamt when I was drowning, no, I was being swallowed by this mystical, magical ground that felt like the body of a woman filled with jelly and custard," he gently breathed in her ear, stealthily slipping his hand underneath her nightie. She stifled. "You mean pudding," she muffled and tightened her knees together. Lester sighed, "every day, it's as if I have just met you," he quivered. "How can a man love a woman, like a tree loves its apples," he soft-soaped. His tongue slurped her neck, stroking her lightly. Vera melted; her body had conceded defeat. He sensed it and mischievously toyed with her.
She braced for an impact and winced. "Shhhh! You will disturb the cat," he muttered obstinately.
Vera salaciously bit her lips and waited for the impact. He meticulously moved his body back and forth. She was all over the place, constricting her harmonious tone to that of a crushed sparrow. He breathed haggardly, fighting for composure. His tongue was in pursuit of her ear; he started to speak in tongues within an instant.
"Two hearts can never be one without the loss of the other. I surrender mine to yours. The source of my desires, the mother of all beauties." Vera puffed and gasped for air.

After a long haul, Lester stifled and became motionless. He held her like a tick, stuck to a steer, she wriggled, and he gently breathed into her ear. "Can I say hello again," He steadfastly spurred her with short, smooth grinds? She sensed a sudden new burst of energy and obsequiously obliged.

The alarm clock rang. Vera was startled, and she wriggled, startled, "I gotta go." She yelled, pushing him away. He was astonished and gasping for breath.

"Umm, Vera," He stammered as he stepped forward, suddenly his legs wobbled, sending him staggering backward in disbelief.

"The floor is slippery," he convinced himself.

"Moritz will be here in about 10mins. I still have to pack my bags. Will you help me get my shoes, please, and my glasses."

Vera spoke nonchalantly. He ignored her, "what's with this broken clock. Do you know what you are doing to me right now?" He rattled.

"I got no idea. What I do know is, I gotta go."

"You are freezing me out." He screamed.

"In what way, my darling, calm down, get some ice."

"Come on!

You know what I mean. I was almost there," he protested bitterly.

"Get me my shoes, will you," she repeated, ignoring his pleas.

"The alarm clock is 30 minutes behind. I adjusted it, I'm telling you," he rumbled, desperately trying to convince her.

"Ok, be nice," she walked to the bed and pretended to pull her skirt up. Lester grinned and ran into the bathroom to get some oil. At that moment, the doorbell rang. "Oops, gotta go," she shouted, adjusting her clothing. "When I get back, see to it that the clock is fixed" Lester looked bewildered as he stood in the middle of the bedroom, unable to move.

"How long are you going to be away, my love?" He vented. She just smiled, "I want to find you the way you are. Will you move before we wake up the kids? Hurry." He followed her in quick steps nagging, and still naked. "There is no justice in this house." Vera abruptly turned around. "Lester, cover yourself! Moritz is outside." He ran back and grabbed a pair of sheets, and wrapped them around his body.

Vera looked elegant! She was wearing a navy suit with a pink shirt. Lester, lascivious, gazed at her. "You look amazing! I could marry you again and again."

"Thank you, love, you don't look bad yourself," she slyly giggled.

"You are right to go and do what you have to do. Don't work yourself too hard? I need you back, the same way you left," he softly muffled and kissed her on the lips. The doorbell rang again.

"Doorbell," a tiny voice shouted, that was Niklaas, their ve year old son. "Shush," Vera signaled to Lester as she

tiptoed down the stairs.

Chapter 2

Moritz was a short bald man with a wide smile. He was a close companion and worked as Vera's assistant. Their broadcasting company based in the city of Cologne was one of the largest in Germany.

They had traveled extensively together, covering news from the Tsunamis in Asia to interviewing some of the world's biggest stars. Witty and creativity had made Vera become a household name in the journalism industry. Her beauty and demeanor had dismantled fortified barriers. She had managed to score an interview with one of the most feared goal minders of the 20th century, the legendary fearsome goalkeeper Oliver Kahn.

„What's with all the mist."
„Strange indeed," Moritz replied.
„Why do you think he specifically asked us to interview him so early in the morning," she asked curiously. Moritz cleared his throat, peeping at the traf c light through his spectacles.
„Well, this guy has the same routine every day for the past twenty years. He has never missed a single training. He has never gotten sick."
„Never," she repeated his words.
„Yes! Never, ever," he replied calmly and continued. „He is highly disciplined, always punctual, a fantastic

individual. He lives for football. He eats football.

In general, he is the epitome of a football god. On the eld or during training, he's the brains behind the whole team. The most impressive goalkeeper ever. His bulky hulk figure intimidates most strikers, and his strength of character makes him a great leader of the group. He wakes up at 4 am each day and goes for a 10km run."

"Wow, are all soccer players like him."

"No one can match his tenets."

"I wonder how the wives of footballers can handle that kind of dedication."

"Oh! I don't think they mind basking in the glory and fame with the kind of money involved. While dad runs around, chasing a bouncing ball, filled with air," he responded with laughter."

"What's so remarkable or extraordinary about him, that Hans wants us without fail to talk to him."

"I thought I just said it. Oliver Kahn is a typical example of a German man, big, strong, guarded by a fortress of an impenetrable mentality. He has never granted anyone an interview. He is extremely private, and he is the best in the world."

Vera scoffed, "he reminds me more of Stef Graf, only a bit more aggressive and scary."

"True to some extend, he once famously said, If I play, I try to concentrate on producing my best."

"Uhhh! And I'm supposed to be his number one fan," she quipped.

On the flight to Munich, Vera could not focus on deciding on her approach. An overzealous star-struck fan stared at her with unblinking eyes, reeking of alcohol and flammable subsbstances. Vera nervously

adjusted her clothing. He looked disheveled with long unkempt hair. His worn out brown leather jacket had skull stickers on it. His small eyes glowed as he weirdly peered at her, forcing his eyebrows to look like a dry millipede.
He beamed with delight and awe at the sight of her expensive jewelry. She pretended to read some notes, but she could feel his gaze scrutinizing her.
She tried to ignore his gawking and rubbernecking expressions, which made her angry and uncomfortable. He took out his phone and googled her name. A page appeared full of her images.
He scrolled on his phone, grinning and burping as he excitedly rubbed on one of the pictures on the screen. Vera looked around for assistance, but the aisle was empty, and Moritz was already in a deep sleep. She took a short breath and decided to engage the pervert in a conversation. "You seem to be well versed about my lifestyle Mr." He grinned, "a junkie knows everything except himself,"
he stated and chuckled.
Vera was annoyed, "Excuse me, I should say your behavior is unacceptable and abnormal. If you don't, stop! I shall report you to the authorities. You could go to jail for that." Immediately he slipped his phone into his jacket and gave her a threatening look.
"Me jail, not again, no, no," he spoke with a heavy Russian accent, which gave her chills. The plane jerked, and she jolted closer to him. He grinned, revealing his gold platted teeth covered in a tainted rust layer. "You are beautiful, and you smell of sweet orgasm." He licked his lips. Vera was angry and shocked. Before she could retaliate, the air hostess approached them.

"Hello! Ms. Bars, are you ok?" She asked with a stern look. Vera's expression said it all. "We have another free seat right at the front. Would you follow me please," the air hostess asked kindly." She hurriedly gathered her papers and grabbed her bag without taking another look at the strange passenger.

"Ms. Bars, did you know that at 1000 km/h, a flightless bird will never taste airborne." She just smirked. "Goody-goody, see you in Munich," he shouted after her.

She sat down and drank a glass of cold water, still feeling upset about the weird man's behavior. She could not stop wondering about the arrogance of the man. Recently she had read comments about her from obsessed fans. She had reoccurring vivid memories about celebrity women stalked, harassed, and eventually killed by unknown assailants. Her body becomes cold. She was numb and afraid.

The thought of her kids frightened her. She wished Lester was around. "He could put some of his martial arts to test," she murmured. After what seemed like an eternity, the plane touched down. She briskly moved to the front and, as if she was mad, sped out of the airport. Moritz was struggling to catch up with her. He hurried after her in confusion. She settled down as soon as she got into their designated vehicle.

"What was that about?" Moritz queried.

Vera held her forehead, with her eyes closed. Moritz was troubled. "Did I miss something," he asked calmly. "If you don't feel comfortable about doing the interview, we could cancel it," he stuttered. She remained quiet, did not say a word for a while.

Eventually, she sighed heavily and got out of the car.
She paced the crowded pavement in search of the culprit. Moritz was speechless! He observed her skeptically and was hesitant to confront her. He figured it must have been a personal issue and didn't want to worsen the situation. Without a word, she jumped back into the car and was herself again. "Just a mild headache, my apologies." She sighed.
"So Oliver Kahn, the great Kahn, you said." Moritz was speechless. She stared at him, and they locked eyes for a while. He reluctantly searched for his folder in confusion.
They drove up to the gate and found Jonas, the cameraman, and Jens, his assistant, waiting with their gear. They had driven overnight and looked exhausted. Oliver Kahn was standing in the courtyard, holding a liter of vitamin juice. He was wearing his traditional goalkeeper attire.
Bold white pinstripes across the front and top of the shoulders, with black shorts. White Socks and giant size Adidas predator ground cleats. He resembled a soccer terminator. He stretched his corrugated flipper hands, giving Vera a solid bumpy grip.
"Whoa, I don't expect that round rubber thing to escape such gauntlet hands," she uttered, and he just laughed. "Welcome to Bayern. The last time I saw you was during the October fest," he roared.
"Oh! Yes, I was there! You did notice me," she answered, smiling.
"I'm aware of a lot of things, Ms. Bars. Should we start?" He pointed to the garden table and led the way. It was an extremely unusual event for Vera. She did her best to be splendor, and he was candor. One thing that

he emphasized was that his days at Karlsruher SC were what shaped his mindset before he transferred to the mighty Bayern Munich. He was exceptionally joyful when he talked of his achievements on the eld.

He discussed in depth his vision for Bayern Munich and his ambition to be at the helm of Bayern in the near future. He laughed hilariously at an incident where Samuel Kuffuor resuscitated him after he got knocked unconscious. He glowed as he talked about his passion for winning and for the love of the sport. The interview scheduled to last thirty minutes went well beyond two hours.

"What a lovely fellow," Moritz finally spoke as they got into the car. Meanwhile, back home, Lester, with his chiseled body, had Niklaas on his back and his little daughter Aya hanging on his neck while he did push-ups on the kitchen floor.

"Ninety-four, ninety- ve," both kids shouted in chorus.

"Come on, dad, ninety-six, four more," cheered Niklaas.

"Yeah, dad, four more," repeated Aya. Lester dipped the kids up and down with ease like flies.

"And a hundred, Niklaus screamed. "You made it, thirty seconds break, and then setups." Hold on, guys, I need to breathe a bit." He complained. Aya, show me how many setups you can do. Come on?" He urged her. "On my count, let's go."

"But papa, I prefer dancing," she replied, running towards the stereo.

"Oh no, dancing," he grumbled.

"Yes, I want to dance," she insisted.

"Yeah, me too, papa," added Niklaas.

"Ok, fine, you guys win, but on one condition." "And what's

that," asked Aya.

"Y'all "Y'all gotta eat your cereals, and it's salad day today. Aya and Niklaas didn't move; they just stared at each other. They hated papa's salad. "Chicken is part of the salad, right?" Niklaas asked cunningly.

"And tomatoes, with cucumber and some eggs," shouted Aya.

Lester looked at them menacingly and roared as he moved towards them. Whoever I catch first does the house chores.

Aya and Niklaas knew what was coming. They scattered around the house yelling and howling with Lester pursuing them.

"Papa, you are too slow; Papa is a chameleon, you can- not catch me," Aya teased him as she struggled to climb the stairs.

"I am paw patrol on roller skates," expressed Niklaas. After a wild round of chasing each other. Lester crouched in the middle of the lounge, breathing heavily. "Okay, guys, you won, time out, come on out, let's quench our thirst." "Orange juice would do for me, thank you," shrieked Niklaas from the pantry room."

"I will go for apple juice! And a cherry pie," responded Aya.

"Hey, you need to watch your weight!"

"No worries, I got mama's genes," she boasted.

"Hallo! What is that supposed to mean, princess?

"It means she snores like a cat." Niklaas blurted.

"I don't snore. Cats don't snore. I don't snore at all. I love cats." She said, fuming. "I know you peed in bed not long ago, she added.

"Be careful what you say, or else this will land on your pretty face and turn it into a dumpster."

"Come on! Hey guys, be nice to one another. Niklaas, you only have one sister, don't you forget. You better treat her unique, and Aya, you only have one brother, be nice to him. Unless if you want me to leave you both at your Oma's place." The two kids shook their heads in disapproval.

After they drove off from the interview, Vera and her crew sat inside an Italian restaurant. They still had six hrs to kill before they caught their flight back home. Moritz decided to be hilarious.

"When I am on the field, everyone is my enemy. My only friend is a ball." He mimicked Oliver Kahn.

"I'm as hard as dry bread," Vera, said coughing.

"And my teammates know me when I get angry, I'm destructive," recited Jonas with a chuckle. Vera excused herself and went outside to make a call home. The moment she stepped out, a sudden gust of wind blew, messing up her hair. She quickly turned away to avoid further damage. At that moment, she caught sight of the disheveled man, who had abused her on the plane. She was startled, and she swiftly took a step back into the restaurant. The man jumped into a waiting taxi, and as it drove by, he turned his head slightly without looking at her. Vera was shaken. She did not know what to think.

Moritz had been watching her from a distance, approached her feeling concerned.

"You distraught Vera, is everything ok." He asked. She sighed.

"I'm not sure, but something seems strange. There was a man on the plane that kind of spooked me. And now I have just seen the same man, standing right there, watching me."

"What?" Exclaimed Moritz as he stepped forward and started looking around frantically.

"Are you positively sure that someone is following us? Do you think you have a stalker? Is that why you acted weirdly at the airport this morning? Why didn't you say something? Should I call the police? Vera was beside herself, agitated by the situation.

She frowned and waved him off. "Maybe it's nothing, just a coincidence." She said hastily.

Moritz did not take the situation lightly. It greatly disturbed him.

The thought of having a stalker was upsetting and dangerous.

"Perhaps it's fatigue, maybe it's all in my head," she desperately tried to assure him. "I'll join you in a minute. Let me make a quick phone call." As she took out her phone, Moritz wandered away, not convinced by her explanation.

"Hey, I miss you guys," Vera said with a strained voice.

"We miss you too, mum," shouted Aya and Niklaus at the same time. "Ok, guys, away with you, let me talk to my wife. Lester shooed them out.

"Hi, there, are you feeling alright? You sound nervous. Did Mr. Kahn scare you? You know your husband is a fifth dan black belt. Are you also aware I am capable of ripping someone's nose out?" „I got a gun, no worries."

"How did it go?" Lester asked.

"He has huge hands and Panda feet," she yelled.

"I miss you fourfold," she continued. "I miss you fourfold."

"I said it first," whined Vera."

"I said it better." Lester protested.

"What has more than a hundred legs and moves like a

snail," he joked. "A millipede, why do you ask?" Are you planning on feeding on decaying vegetation?"
"No, I'm carnivorous. Which animal dies during copulation?"
"That's a hard one. How does it die? Does it die because it gets crushed by the excited partner or because of natural exhaustion?" Both, she replied.
"Got it," he snapped.
"Got what?"
"Arev," he boasted.
"What the hell is Arev?"
"Hahaha," he laughed, "spell it backward."
"Oh! You, cheating again."
"I just won what, was the bet again? Did you say I do whatever I want? Hey! come home, and we can watch The Full monty going full moon." He screamed excitedly on the phone.
"You naughty skinny-legged Ostrich," she teased him, and he let out a wolf cry.
"Yah yah crying wolf." She mocked him. "Will be home soon. I cannot wait to hear that wolf cry again."
â€ I will be waiting in the shadows, seething and hissing, watching and planning,â€ he rapped over the phone.
Vera arrived back in Cologne way past dinner time. She insisted on taking a cab instead of Moritz driving her home. As she rode in the taxi, she pondered what she should get her parents for their 40th anniversary. She was the only child and was extremely close to her father. Her mother had become disheartened and demoralized after the miscarriage of her would be, younger sister during a car accident. She had disconnected herself from the rest of the world. Her father had bought a house in the middle of nowhere to appease her.

Once a successful tall, beautiful businesswoman, she had transformed into an empty shell of herself. Panic attacks and mood swings took control of her life. Nonetheless, when she was level-headed, she was the most sympathetic mother you'll ever come across. Vera felt depressed and distressed at the
thought of the pain her mum was experiencing. She was glad to have a compassionate and caring husband in Lester.

He was her pillar, her strength, her protector, and above all, he had brought happiness and fulfillment to her family. The taxi rolled to a stop. Only the patio light was on, and the street
was empty and silent. She felt a fantastic fresh breeze brush against her face. The leaves rustled, and the muffled sounds of the mysteries of the night stepped out. A ball of mist crossed the road and disappeared among the bushes. An old owl shrieked, followed by an eerie sound.

Vera jolted, causing her to freak out. She rushed towards the door with the keys dangling in her hands.

Her wealthy neighborhood of Marienburg was situated about five kilometers from the city center. It was a quiet, peaceful suburb surrounded by spacious, huge beautiful houses and carefully trimmed gardens. During the day, many residences took walks along the well-manicured boulevard strip.

She felt safe once inside the comfort of her own

home. Moritz called immediately to check if she had gotten home safely.

"Thanks, Moritz, soon I'II will be snoring. I wish you a goodnight. Bye." She smiled when she saw a note stuck on the fridge. She plucked it out and   poured herself a glass of chocolate. She leaned against the kitchen sink with her lips pouted and began to read.

"My current and futuristic wife, an oasis of beauty filled with abundance, richness, and serenity.
I bow down to your godly body covered in sweet frozen chocolate that can only melt on my golden tongue. A soft touch creates a wave of flesh that ripples, sending undetectable signals straight to my well-coiled antenna, giving me a well-deserved shock that even Einstein's hair will strengthen up. I might not be a scientist, but I can unlock and tangle your veins until our blood type is O. Right now, I need a blood transfusion. Your absence has made me weak. Death awaits. I am a minute away from suffocating. I desperately need your divine assistance."
Signed L.B

Vera smiled mildly. She felt sweat forming on her back. Her hands put down the chocolate drink and poured herself a red wine to calm her nerves. Then she recalled the promise she had given Lester earlier that morning. A smile crept across her face, with her blue eyes blinking. She sighed and gulped her wine. Out of excitement, she threw away her jacket and galloped upstairs, forgetting that the kids were are asleep.

Suddenly she remembered and taciturnly called out his name, "Lester, your savior is here. She yanked the door open and three terrifying snoring bunnies greeted her. She sulked and squeezed herself between the kids. For a while, she lay wide awake, listening to her family snoozing. The thought of going to her mother's place gave her nightmares.

In the morning, Lin, their weekend maid, was busy folding and ironing clothes. She was a tall lady for an Asian person, with big eyes and a wide friendly smile.

Chapter 3

Birds chirped as the blue sky slowly opened up, and the sun gradually raised its temperature. "Good morning Mrs. Bars. How was your sleep?" She said, turning around to face her.

"Hi Lin, very well, thank you. You are here early?"

"Yes, because I thought you might need my help before you drive to your parents."

"Very thoughtful of you, thank you. It's going to be a long weekend. Do you have any plans?" Vera inquired.

"Not really; I'll be busy with my children. I hardly see them. Maybe I'll take them somewhere interesting."

"Breakfast is ready," shouted Lester from the kitchen.

"There goes the bear," Vera yelled. "You guys owe me an apology.

"And why is that?" Aya asked.

"Oh, you playing dumb, little sis. Why were you in my bed last night?

"Oops, I don't remember how I slept, mama. Papa was supposed to carry me to my bed."

"I had a blackout," Lester shouted from the back.

"I wasn't sleeping, mama. I heard your footsteps. You were running upstairs, and I got scared, so I covered myself," Niklaas chuckled.

"You ran up the stairs. Was a ghost chasing you, or were you running after something? "Lester teased her.

"Nope, none of that. I was tired. I wanted to sleep, and

I kept my promise." She said sarcastically. Lester rolled his eyes and rubbed his chin.

"My apologies, I'll deal with the situation accordingly at Oma's house." He gave her a naughty kiss on the forehead and tickled her. "Whose turn is it to give grace," Aya interrupted them.

"It's your turn Aya, don't try to be smart," Niklaas smirked.

"Let's all hold hands. "Our Father, thank you for putting tasty food on the table. I know papa cooked it, but I also know you gave him the strength to wake up. I have nothing to say about my mother because she is always amazing to me, and I love her so much. My brother Niklaas sometimes is a bit of a jerk.

Please, Lord, do not let him make fun of me. And now I want to thank myself for this beautiful life of being allowed to eat a lot of ice cream. Amen."

"Amen," they repeated after her.

"Nice prayer Aya. I love you too," Vera said. Gimme a kiss."

"I love you too, mum," cried out Niklaas.

"And no one has a love for me," scoffed Lester. "I packed the bags, I prepared delicious food, and I still don't get any love.

"But papa, you are a man. Love is only for women," Aya snarled.

"Who told you that? Your mama? I need love too." Lester humorously demanded.

"This is what we are going to do. As soon as we get to Oma's house, we will show papa plenty of love. We will show him with tidbit love and feed him some fresh strawberries and cream." Vera lauded.

"Yip, ice cream mama, chocolate or vanilla," Aya

shrieked. Lester bit his lip and turned his eyes upward. "I'll take the bags out to the car. Are you going to give me a hand, Niklaas?"

"Sure, daddy, on my way." They left Vera and Aya debating about which avor was the tastiest.

Around 11 am, they made their way towards Flensburg.

It was a town situated in the North of Hamburg, about 600 kilometers away from Cologne. Vera's father had bought a house in a little village called Olderup, which had approximately four hundred people. The weather was perfect for a long drive. The temperatures were mild, and the sun kept playing hide and seek with the clouds. Lester loved his Audi AQ.

"Niklaas, Niklaas," he called out his son.

"What engine is this?"

"It's a V6 engine papa, 8-speed automatic transmission, allwheel drive." Lester smiled proudly. He looked at his wife and nodded his head. "That's my son." Vera snared at him and smirked. She called out Aya. "Aya, my princes."

"Yes, mama."

"Give me three sentences using us."

"We Love you. We believe in you."

"Hahaha!" Vera chuckled, "one more, come on."

"We are a beautiful family," Aya purred.

"Yeah, gimme ve, my princess, that's my daughter." She stared at her husband and nodded. Lester took a deep breath.

"Son, are you ready."

"Let's do this, daddy."

Lester began to sing in a deep voice.

"Last night was bright
The stars were shining
Niklaas joined in a low pitched voice.

Last night was bright.
The stars were, shining.
We wanted to play (chorus)
We didn't have a ball.

Last night was bright.
The stars were, shining.

We wanted to eat
There was no food

So what did we do - son

We bought knick-knacks
We bought chocolates,

We bought knick-knacks
We bought chocolates

"Hold on, Hold, not so quick, this song doesn't exist.
That is unfair. Vera heckled them.
"Now it does exist right Nik."
"We wrote it yesterday with daddy ma," he answered
quickly.
"Mum, we need our song," cried out Aya, "or else I'm
moving to papa's side." They burst out laughing.
"Don't worry, darling. We won't let them win so easily.
Poetically describe me." Lester swelled his chest out.
"An oasis of innocence filled with abundance richness
and serenity, hidden behind a fortress of a waterfall."

"Ooh, not bad." Vera loved it.
"I love you too." He responded. "And it's your turn."
Vera smiled shyly and melted.

As soon as the kids fell asleep, Vera began to nod off. Lester put the car in cruise control and switched the music to his favorite band, "Seed." He glanced at the speedometer. He was doing 240 kilometers per hour. He felt proud. Usually, the motorway is abuzz with race drivers. But this time, no one came close to overtaking him. He peeked at his pretty wife and appreciated her innocent beauty. Through the review mirror, he could see Aya and Niklas's heads slumped awkwardly
at the back. He took a deep breath and sand along to Augenbling.

Chapter 4

Lester had a rough upbringing. His father passed away when he was four years old. Soon after that, his mother took her own life because of depression. He grew up in a foster home and had to fight his way up. His wife and kids and Vera's parents were the only families in his life. He had chosen to take up Vera's surname after their wedding. There were times he wished his parents were alive. They could have been proud of

his achievements. His wish was to raise a big family. "At least seven kids," he whispered with a broad smile on his face. His thoughts were distracted when he noticed Vera twitching and rattling as she slept. She was in a labyrinth of conspicuous dreams. He gave her a nudge, and she woke up with a jump.

"Whoa, that must have been a scary nightmare?" He sneered.

"Here, take a sip. Are you alright?" She looked dazed and worried.

"Oh, I am glad you are here," she whispered, wiping her mouth.

"I just had the most dreadful dream ever," she stuttered.

"What happened?" He asked curiously, rubbing her forehead. She cast a doubtful look at the back seat and beamed. "Umm! I was hitchhiking from planet to planet trying to bring back home our lost dogs." She said.

"Dogs! What dogs? We have no dogs," he exclaimed.

"Well, in the dream, I was going after five dogs, and as I was about to catch them, they would suddenly melt and vanish.

"Okay, that's interesting, go on."

"Well, I started searching for them, and each time I got closer, they would jump to the next planet. I had to struggle to catch a ride and follow. I ran through snowy mountains, huge underwater caves, across the desert. And when I tried to turn back, Aya would urge me to go on. At one point, I recognized that my mother was helping them to escape."

"Uh, now it's getting interesting the whole family is in there," he chuckled.

"Then, uh from nowhere, Niklaus appeared among the dogs, he thought we were playing hide and seek."

Lester turned his eyes around in circle. "What has my son got to do with that?" He snapped. "Did you managed to catch these dogs?"

"No because every time I blinked a new planet would pop up.

They were five planets in total and at one point, the dogs separated and jumped onto different planets."

"Umm you mean you had five dogs on five different planets.

"Yeah that's right. I got tired and I sat down by the bridge overlooking a castle. When I looked up to the sky the dogs had disappeared. They were no more dogs. But what was crazy was, all my family member's faces were popping up on each cloud."

"Whose faces?"

"Your face, my mother's face, my father's face, my aunt's face, Aya and Niklaas's faces, but my face was missing.

I want to know why?" She smirked.

Lester grimaced and pouted. He nodded his head teasingly. "I'm listening."

"The funny things is, I was shouting and complaining. I don't know to who. I was screaming, why is my face not on the cloud. I want my face on the cloud. I began to jump up, thinking I could fly and join you guys, but I couldn't. I attempted to jump on a kite being flown by jackals but it was too small, and I fell into the water," she giggled.

"Umm!" Lester lightly nodded his head.

"That's when it struck me, something strange was happening.

The more effort I made, the more you guys moved further away. So I stopped trying and you all came closer to me. I was gesturing to you, I don't remember what I was saying. Suddenly there was a wild fierce gust of wind, with a ball of fire in the middle. And it just literally came and blew everyone away. I didn't know what to do. I was hysterical and out of control, I think that's when you poked me."

Lester glanced at her weirdly. "From what I saw, you did put up a good fight. I am glad you are willing to die for your family. But I am afraid, that wouldn't make your dream a good movie."

"I hate scary dreams, nightmares are not cool," she fumed.

"The last dream I had," Lester said as he switched on the indicators, and pulled into service station. "Was when you were filling up the fuel tank and cleaning the windshield."

"Papa, can I get an ice cream," Aya yawned waking up. They were both startled. "Huh how long have been

awake, next time the moment you open your little eyes, you shout! I'm awake, okay." Lester gnashed teeth. "Papa, I didn't hear anything, and it's not my business." "What,
little princess, you playing with me."
"Come, love, let's see what they have got in there." Vera stepped out of the car and opened the passenger door. "I am still talking, Lester rumbled. "Keep it for later." Vera quietened him. She and Aya swung their hands and walked towards the minimarket.

By the time they arrived in Olderup, the sun was almost setting. Vera's parents lived in the remote part of Olderup. Their house was in the middle of nowhere, surrounded by thick bushes. "Come people up, up. We are almost there. Your best behavior is demanded from now on until we leave. Remember, always be polite and be gentle with your Oma. Please pick up your toys after you finish playing with them. Eat all your food on your plate. And no talking while eating. Aya, no asking too many questions. Niklaas, do what she asks you to do. One more thing, don't forget to switch off the lights after you leave your room." Vera ranted.
Lester turned the car into a small private road. Mr. Bars had converted an old church into a luxurious home. He believed the blood of Jesus and the prayers of many worshippers who had attended the church would protect him and his wife from evil deeds.
Mr. and Mrs. Bars stood in front of the house in anticipation. He had a grey suit and a black shirt. His grayish hair glittered in the light of the headlamps, and his smile revealed white neatly arranged teeth. Mrs. Bars was a tall, slender woman. You could tell during

her days that she must have been a head turner.
She radiated in a dark navy blue satin blouse with black velvet trousers. Her straightforward demeanor and elegant style made her glamorous without being ostentatious. "Wow, is that your mother? Exclaimed Lester. "I must say she's aging backward." He whistled with a grin on his face. "She does give the impression of being dazzling.
I wonder what happened to her," Vera said excitedly. "Maybe she has been reborn again, mama," shouted Niklaas. "Okay, shush! Quite at the back," she said as she adjusted her hair.
The car came to a halt in the driveway. Vera jumped out and embraced her mother. "Mum, you look stunning. I hope I'll look the same when I am your age."
"I feel rehabilitated, gaining strength, my darling," she replied softly. "How are you, my celebrity daughter.
I follow your reporting on the news."
"I try to do my best, mama. Look at your grandkids." The mother giggled, "Oh my, my is that Aya. She reminded me of you when you were a kid. Come and say hello to your Oma." Aya and Niklaas rushed to their Oma like toddlers. Vera turned to her father. "Hello, Papa, the only handsome gentleman I know, besides Lester, of course." She opened her arms and hugged him. "Jumbo bwana, jumbo," he replied. The only African words he knew. "So good to see you, papa." Lester cleared his throat, feeling unnoticed.

"I'm Lester, the beautiful lady's husband," he said as he stepped forward. The father chuckled. "You never cease to amaze me, Mr uh, Bars,"
and he laughed again. "First, you take my daughter and

then you steal my name." Lester cracked up hilariously. "I just wanted to blend in, and your name sounds powerful, Mr. Bars. It's a name that suits a King. I can promise you one thing though, Sir, your name is in good safe hands." "How are you, Mr. Robert Bars." Lester played the fool. "How are you, Mr. Lester Bars, Vera's father yelled, chuckling. Lester continued. "It's always my pleasure to see you, Sir.
He said, shaking his hand. Thank you again for bringing Vera into this world."
"Well, it wasn't that hard; wait a minute, was it?" And they both laughed. Lester turned to Mrs. Bars and bowed his head.
"We are back again, this time with plenty of empty stomachs. Your love, your cooking, and your fantastic hospitality have driven us here." He spoke calmly and with respect. She grinned from ear to ear.

"You are not fooling me, and I haven't cooked in ages." Vera and her Father walked arm in arm back into the house. The kids jostled for the attention of their grandmother. Lester was left alone offloading the luggage. Without warning, it had suddenly become dark and chilly.

Chapter 5

The building stood like a gigantic sleeping robot waiting to be reactivated. Lester felt uneasy at the thought that this was once a church. Inside the house, the furniture arrangement and the placement of African sculptures and suspended chandeliers were ingenious. It was done in an elaborate way and with great skill.

The beautiful occupants were ecstatic and generous to their visitors. Oma was playing with her grandkids as she showered them with presents and love. Mr. Bars and Lester had insisted on preparing dinner for the family. Vera was upstairs unpacking and folding their belongings. Lester laughed loudly before clearing his throat. He was in a deep conversation with his father in law.

"We have been thinking of purchasing a country home, somewhere not so isolated. You have a great place here. I wouldn't give it up for anything. But I think Vera and I need you to be closer to you. You know, stay in one big house as a big family. I haven't discussed it with her, by the way. She misses you guys, and the kids would love it." Mr. Bars scoffed, "we would visit from time to time, but to live with you all, no. That would be catastrophic. You know my wife can be moody at times. I wouldn't want my grandkids to think their Oma is a lunatic. That would be devastating to them."

"Uhh, I understand," Lester answered, rubbing his chin. "I did not say never, but If somehow, my wife suggests it. I would give it a second thought." Mr. Bars emphasized. The phone rang, distracting him. He looked at his watch in disbelief.
"Who is calling at this time of the hour?
"It's only 8 pm, Sir," Lester replied.
"Well, this is a church. We are in bed by 7 pm."
"I'll get it," Vera shouted. She picked up the phone, but there were only inaudible whoosh sounds.
"Hello, hello, anyone there? No one is responding, daddy," she yelled from upstairs.
The moment she placed the phone down, it rang again.

She waited for it to ring a couple of times more. "Pick up the phone, Vera," her father shouted.
"Hello, Bars residence," she answered. A sweet voice came through from the other side. "Oh, that's not Monica's voice, is that you, Vera."
"Aunt Ruth," Vera screamed. "What a pleasant surprise that you called."
"It would be pleasant for me too if someone could come and get me. I think your father forgot to pick me up. I am here at the Flensburg Bahnhof," (train station), she stuttered in a soft sweet old voice. "Will you please hurry and take me away from this cold."
"Aunt Ruth, you mean you are around. Oh, that's great news. I had no idea you were coming. Now listen carefully, aunt Ruth, go and sit in the cafe opposite the station. I'll be there in thirty minutes, okay. There is only one cafe. I'm on my way; see you just now." Vera put the phone down and rushed downstairs excitedly.
"Mama, Papa, you forgot to pick up aunt Ruth. She's

waiting at the station as we speak." Her father looked at her, confused. "Your aunt is around. She didn't tell me she was coming. Maybe she called your mother. Monica did you know Ruth was arriving today," Mr. Bars asked his wife. Mrs. Bars looked at him with a smirk on her face. "Well, I'll go and pick her up then. She must be freezing,"
Vera remarked.
"I'll come with you," Lester suggested.
"Me too, mum," Aya shouted from the lounge.
"No, no guys, stay right where you are. It's alright, and it's only a minute's drive. Aya, you keep on playing with your Oma, and hun, make sure the food is lekker."

She kissed her husband, her father, and hugged her two kids. She knelt close to her mother and said, "I'll be back in about 45mins, take care of my babies." She kissed her on the forehead and left.
"Hey, Vera, can I have a quick word with you upstairs, please."
"Now."
"Yes, now, it's important." Lester insisted.
"It won't take too long, love, just a word of advice," Lester begged her. He pulled her back upstairs, and they made love passionately. She got up, ran down the stairs, grabbed the keys from the holder mounted on the wall by the side of the door, and disappeared outside.
"Drive safely, hun," Lester shouted through the door. When she was outside, she realized she had opted for her mother's convertible BMW car. She hesitated because she knew no one was allowed to drive her mum's car. But she went against it.
Even though it was dark and getting chilly, she dropped

down the roof and glided the sleek ride towards Flensburg. She loved cruising in drop-tops and was hoping her mom won't come out to greet them when she returned with her aunt. The car was one of her most desired possession.

She had acquired it fifteen years ago, and it still looked brand new. Vera loved her aunt. She was full of humor, and they shared a lot of her secrets. She's the one who had hooked her up with Lester when she had visited her ten years ago. She had attended a fitness course Lester was coaching.

"Well, the good thing is, you have a health conscious man in the house. Who'll not let you ballon into a Yokozuna," she had joked. She smiled coyly at the thought.

Further ahead she noticed dark fog spreading across the road. She pondered whether to close the top. At that moment a mysterious fog swept across partially blinding her view. She was confused and nervous. The fog quickly melted into thin air. Through an eyelet, a camouflaged vehicle with no visible headlamps suddenly flashed her, as it sped past going in the opposite direction. Someone swung a bottle out and it smashed on the windscreen of her car. Vera veered off the road and struggled with the steering wheel trying to avoid crashing into a signpost.

She was shell-shocked and traumatized. It took a while for her to consume what had just transpired. She got out of the car and cursed at the perpetrators and their truck. "Headless goblins, sons of witches, cursed cockroaches, dim darks. What a stupid crate of a car."

She was furious. She moved around, examining her

car. A conspicuous spider web spread on the window screen's left corner. There were shiny pieces of broken bottles scattered on the road. She tried to clean up and throw away the more significant bits from the road.

When she arrived at the station aunt, Ruth was having a conversation with a group of young men.
"There she is. I warned you she's gorgeous." "Uh that's Vera Bars, the tv presenter," shouted one of them cheerfully. Vera felt uncomfortable as other guests turned and glanced at her. After the usual group chat, she dragged her half tipsy aunt away.
"You haven't changed one-bit, auntie, you remember you introduced me to a wonderful man.
Who happens to be my husband. I am a married woman and very satisfied." Vera gloated with her arm around her. Could you stop trying to hook me up? It embarrasses me." She chirped.
"Um, I glad I played a part; satisfaction is a great deal achieved by a few." She burped and peered at her. "The best fruit is the one that is never ripe." Aunt Ruth quipped.
"It watches as others become too ripe and get eaten by birds or fall off. When its turn comes, by the time you notice it. It's already too late. It would have been covered by dark marks from the inside out. Keep shining, my dear, put yourself out there, observe and maintain. When the time comes, a single wrinkle will resemble a thousand flies."
"Huh," Vera squirmed.

"You traveled light this time," she changed the subject.
"I noticed you only have a small handbag.

"No, I didn't; them boys have my luggage." Vera turned around. To her amazement, three guys were wheeling her aunt's suitcases. "You still have a lot to learn, my dear. But, no worries, I'll make sure that you'll get there, as long as I'm your aunty. Did Rob tell you I have finally decided to move in with them?"
"You mean mum and dad."
"Yes, my brother and your mother, after years of courting me." Vera was excited about the news.
"No one said anything about it."
"I know because I didn't tell them."
"You mean you are visiting and going to stay for good. You are not just going to leave, cool." She belted out laughing.
"Uh, well, something in that direction, she admitted.

Vera was amused. "Auntie, you are one amazing woman and wild too."
They loaded the luggage and made their way home. Vera drove safely, afraid the window screen might break. Her aunt was narrating her adventures, jumping from one story to the next.
"I met this wonderful handsome man, almost the same age as me. Yes, he was a tourist, moving around Europe, so I decided to join him. It was a spontaneous decision. But it turned out to be the greatest holiday I ever had."
Vera listened attentively. "Where is he now?"
"Oh, he ran away back to his home country," she giggled."
"He ran away. Why?"
"Brute force of nature, I call it."
Vera looked at her awkwardly, not sure what she meant.
"Spiritual reasons and family issues, beyond our control,

took him away. He said he is a merman."
"What," and they tittered like little girls.
"You didn't get his number, address, just in case you might want to send him a sea card."
She snickered, "uh, at my age, Nah, I don't do sea pals. Some people are just weird, my dear. You cannot declare to know a man until you have experienced his presence in tranquility."
"Uhh, where is he from?"
Aunty Ruth hesitated, "um, not sure, Congo, Zimbabwe, Maputo."
"Maputo! Vera exclaimed, "isn't that the capital city of Mozambique.
"Yeah, you got it," she yelled.
Vera was curious. "He spoke Portuguese."
"Uhh, yes, he did speak a lot of languages. He was everything a woman wants in a man, smooth talker, intelligent, tall, and handsome, but guess what. We never did it." They roared with laughter.

Vera had tears in her eyes. Her cheeks were hurting. "How did you communicate though, maybe he asked you, and you didn't get it?"
"você é muito bonita!" She answered.
"Aunty, wow, that's pretty good," Vera was lost for words.
"Tell me more."
"Eu quero fazer amor com você," aunty Ruth continued. Vera was blown away. She stared at her in disbelief.
"If a man wants to spice up his marriage, he needs to leave home for the mountains once in a while. He needs to sit on top of a huge stone and observe the eagles' ways. It's something I learned from him." Vera stuttered, but

where did you learn to speak Portuguese."
"If you move around with a deaf and mute person, in the end, you become deaf and mute too," she cackled. "He was on a selfseeking journey. Midlife crises, you call it. And I brought him home nice and clean." "Midlife crisis, I thought you said he was your age." She laughed in a loud, harsh way.
That made Vera even more interested, "How old was he?"
"I don't know your age, I guess."
"Whoa, aunty," they dissolved into laughter."
"Oh, oh aunty," Vera cried out again.
"I like them young. It brings out the youthful spirit in me.
He told me that, open your spiritual eyes, he told me." She mimicked him.
There was a sudden gust of fog swirling above them. "Oh, where did that come from, Vera."
"What," Before she could answer, there was a loud bang. The car swerved to the left and right. Vera screamed. "Wow, what was that?" There was a wobbling noise. "One of the tires burst."
Very frantically managed to gain control and brought the car to a smooth halt, with gritted teeth.
"Are you hurt, aunt?"
"As cool as a cat," she gasped, gazing up to the sky.
"Please let it not be a puncture," Vera pleaded.
"Oh dear, looks like the devil follows me wherever I go," aunty Ruth shrieked. "I've had three consecutive misfortunes since I came back from holiday. Maybe this man cursed me."
She snorted. "And now this."
Vera got out of the car and went to inspect. She was

crouching next to the left front tire, trying to figure out what to do. She had never changed a tire before.

"Well don't just stand there. Get the jack and the spare wheel out," aunty Ruth rattled her. There were reflections of broken glass on the tarred surface. Vera saw the road sign and realized it was almost the same place where she had been forced out of the road.

A police car silently halted behind them, and the officer approached them unnoticed.

"Good evening ladies, we seem to have a puncture, don't we."

They turned around and were relieved to see a policeman. He was tall, well built, and fully equipped for

war. He looked at them and stared at the road ahead. Yeah, some spoiled brats were having a bottle fight. We received numerous complaints from well-concerned citizens." His voice was deep and clear.

"You don't look like a police officer at all, my dear. I could have mistaken you for a football model player." Aunty Ruth said, scrutinizing him. He chuckled shyly, "thank you for the compliments, mum. I did play the sport during my younger years."

"I thought so, and those broad shoulders are not from nothing."

He smiled wildly and asked, "isn't his Mrs. Bars's car right. You must be Vera then," he said, turning his attention to her.

"She is a famous presenter, it'll be an insult if you didn't know who she is." Aunty Ruth pointed out.

"Well I am officer Wenz," he said, extending his hand before crouching next to the tire. Uh, let me have a look.

It's getting late Mrs. Bars would be certainly worried."
He placed the jack underneath the car.
"It's not very often we get such disturbances around
here, this is a peaceful town. Everyone knows and
respects one another. Of course, someone gets out of
hand but not to the point of smashing bottles on the
motorway. That's absurd and inhumane. Who would do
show such an egregious, lunatic thing?
This kind of behavior cause accidents, and motorists
can die from such carelessness. Whoever did this, we
must not allow them to get away with it. We will finally
catch up with them. We've cameras installed all over the
town. As I speak, my colleagues are already combing
through footage from various locations," he disclosed.

Within five minutes, officer Wenz had fixed the tire, and
they were on their way home. Vera was concerned she
would find the kids already in bed, and she assumed she
had missed having dinner with them. She was irked by
the sound of two fire trucks with loud sirens, signaling
them to move out of the way.
"This village is a busy place tonite," aunt Ruth said,
yawning. But Vera didn't respond. Her eyes grew wider
when she saw the trucks turning into the pathway that
led to their house. Aunt Ruth saw the look on her face,
and she became silent. More fire trucks and police cars
were blistering past them. She turned and plowed the
car into the driveway, horror stricken. The whole house
was on fire. She rammed on the brakes so hard that the
windscreen came crashing down. She jumped out of the
car and ran towards the house screaming.

"My family is in there. My kids, where are they? Lester,

Lester, papa, papa," she shouted as she ran. She managed to get past one police officer, but officer Wenz grabbed her from behind. She wriggled free and slipped into the muddy caused by the water from the fire trucks. Officer Wenz held her to the ground as she kicked and screamed.

"My kids are in there, mama, Aya, where are you? Niklaus, Lester, where are you?"

The blaze was intense. It looked as if a gas tank had blown up. Aunty Ruth stood a distance away in distraught, traumatized, sorrow written all over her face. There was a reflection of the blaze burning furiously in her eyes.

"Robert," she said slowly. A loud bang cracked in her head, and she fell.

"They tried everything they could do; no one had a chance. It was too late," Wenz shouted remorsefully at Vera. She moaned and wailed. Her face was covered with tears and mucus.

Officer Wenz felt her pain immensely. He picked her up and carried her away from the burning house.

A crowd had gathered around the perimeter created by the police. Part of the house curved in and smashed into there, causing a massive explosion. Because of the commotion caused by the police sirens, and the noises from the fire trucks, no one noticed that aunt Ruth gripped with shock had fallen on a broken bottle.

She lay there dead with a piece of a sharp bottle protruding through her throat.

The house was completely burnt down. Vera had lost her whole family in a single day. She was devastated. Two of the firefighters had second-degree burns.

After three months of extensive suffering, Vera moved out of their marital house and rented a small apartment in a noisy and busy district. The area was called Zulpicherplatz. It was full of student bars and night spots. Each day was a wild party going on in one of the many bars. The most prominent university in the city of Cologne was only a few hundred feet away. She chose to surround herself with as many disruptions and disturbances as possible. When it was too quiet during the night, she would get up and go for a bicycle ride for hours on some occasions.

And she was only returning during the early hours of the morning. She would sit and sleep on park benches for days in a row.

After about five months, Vera turned up for work to everyone's surprise. She had taken sabbatical leave. A thick layer of aggravated makeup usually covered her facial features. Her manager Krayl was as surprised as everyone else to see her. He sat her down in his office and looked at her for some time. The last time he had seen her was at the funeral. He had been unable to talk to her due to her condition. "Vera, I have known you for a long time. We have achieved many things together. Not only are you a friend, a colleague, but you are also family to me. I value our relationship and the mutual respect everyone has for you.
No, need to rush anything. I want you to take as much time as you wish. I'm not prepared to put you out there so that the whole world can sympathize with you. You are one of my best presenters, and we all miss you dearly. We all have had our challenges, our burdens, our grief.

Sometimes we have found ourselves in bottomless pits, but we have always turned our misfortunes around at the right time."

"I need to be out there, Krayl," she demanded.
He rubbed his broad chin and was silent for a while. "The more I stay locked up, feeling miserable for myself, the crazier I get. I need to take my mind away from all this, to be human again. If you care about it, you have to accept me back as soon as possible. Before I commit suicide," she divulged with tears building in her eyes. Krayl was disturbed by her words. He sighed and spoke quietly.
"There is a project we have been delaying for some time. In two weeks, I should get the go-ahead. And as a friend, I think it will take a great load off your shoulders. Lessen your burden, should I say." Vera listened attentively without saying a word.
It's something that I meant to discuss with you soon," he choked.

"I cannot just be sitting around, grieving. It's driving me nuts. I need to get out and be productive. I'm getting insane. Look at me. I can't be waiting for some miracle to happen." Krayl cleared his throat and hesitated, "how about we have lunch tomorrow at 2 pm, at the Havana Restaurant. You know the one by Barbarossaplatz."
"I haven't been to a normal place in ages," she replied. "I know," he responded softly, "grieving periods will never end, not for anybody. We have to be careful not to grieve ourselves to death." She lifted her head and looked at him. But said nothing. "Terrible things have happened to me, and my family in the past. My parents

are still grief-stricken for the past 35 years. He turned around and gave her his back as if in deep thoughts.

"I have never told anyone this, never. My parents went on holiday and left my little sister with our maid. When they returned and could not find her, they thought she had stolen her and disappeared. But both of them had been mauled by stray dogs. We found her behind our house, in a maize field. A pack of vicious dogs had torn them part." He choked as he spoke, his eyes fixated on the floor.

"Oh, no that was gruesome, horrifying," she stated.

"What a terrible death," she continued.

Krayl sighed somehow, he knew his plan would work.

That day as she walked home, an investigator called her and informed her about the conclusion of their investigation. The motive behind the death of her family members was purely robbery, he said. Between five to six men had managed to gain access into the house and overpowered the occupants. They ransacked the whole place. The kids had died upstairs in bed, and two adults had died of stab wounds. The third victim they

assumed was the mother died of blunt force to the head. One of the attackers was killed during the robbery. The news drove Vera insane. Flashbacks of that night flooded her head. She sat on the carpet distraught with a half-full bottle of Vodka.

Chapter 6

The next day she woke up with a hangover. She remembered the meeting with Krayl. Her head was aching, and she did her best to disguise herself. She was nervous.

She sat silently in Havana restaurant, waiting for Krayl to turn up. Her dark glasses could not conceal her under-eye circles. She did not see Krayl approaching.

"Am I late, or you are just too early," he said as he placed a bunch of papers on the table.

"I had nothing to do, so I've been sitting here for a couple of hours."

"Am I suppose to believe that, you are looking better than yesterday," he chuckled.

"Hahaha," Vera scoffed.

"They have the best paella, Cuban version, without the seafood, really lekker. You should try it," he suggested.

"No, I'll go for uh shrimps in coconut sauce."

"That sounds delicious too, with some fresh bread." They ate their meal quietly. Krayl was a calculated man and he had a penchant for good food. He devoured his food within minutes and drained the cold glass of orange juice in one go. Vera watched him as he wiped his mouth and gasped for air before ordering a glass of white wine. His eyes wandering around in search of nothing. He coughed and straightened his broad shoulders before he embarked on his intentions. With a stern voice he spoke smoothly.

"I'm not going to repeat myself, what has happened has to come to pass. I'm going to send you on a mission. It'll last as long as you do your job accordingly." Vera's eyes widened, "you mean, you are giving me an assignment." "Yes, he said boldly." She silently thanked her god.
"My dream has been answered"
"I'm giving you a chance not only to redeem yourself, but to make peace with your soul, and reclaim your life back."
"I'm prepared for anything, whatever you got for me, I'm in," she mumbled.
"It's kind of an intricate mission, complicated, dangerous," he sighed. "It requires a great deal of awareness and some sense of great responsibility. You'll be in a safe zone though, and you'll be coordinating with your peers in other countries." Her eyes melted, "safe zone, am I going to a war zone," she hissed, her eyes penetrating his soul.
He hesitated, "well, not exactly, but it's a place that the atrocities of war have ravaged, and it's in the process of restoration. Something that you need to overcome yourself."
She breathed heavily and nodded her head. He paused, cleared his throat, and continued, "There are rumors, unheard of, that wicked, inhuman sufferings have occurred in that country. Stuff that you can only see in movies, decapitated heads, mutilated bodies, tortured women. Your mission is to nd out how far true these allegations are. I want a full confirmation about all these uncivilized, primitive, barbaric acts," he grunted. "And where am I going."
"Sierra Leone," his voice bellowed. "I've gathered bits and pieces of what you might need to know," he

continued as he placed a bunch of papers in front of her. "You could leave in two days, is that enough time for you to prepare." She looked at him in surprise, and truthfully answered, "sure, I can even go right now." "Good, that's what I wanted to hear. I'll get Nancy to prepare for your departure. If you need anything else, just give her a call." Vera seemed to be in deep thoughts. Nancy was his longtime secretary. "And uhh

Vera," he interrupted her, "take full advantage of this opportunity. Word is going around. I want you to have a clean slate, harness the power of the moment. You only got one last chance, dive into it, and bring yourself back." Her eyes shot out. She could not understand what he meant before she could ask anything. He continued rumbling, "You are highly skillful in your work, and your ability to penetrate deeply into people's minds is what afforded you this gratitude. Its a jungle out there, and you, you have just made a rewarding move. With you on board, the winds are favorable. "Good luck," he roared. He stared at her for a while and patted her shoulder.
He then got up and maneuvered his way out of the now-packed restaurant.

Vera remained seated for a couple of more hours. She was in deep thoughts. The offer was unexpected, and she was concerned about the subtle meanings he had tried to conceal.
Nonetheless, she was glad she could get away for some time. Unbeknownst to her, Moritz and an unknown accomplice were eagerly waiting for her at a private runway.

"And with the click of the finger the old team is back again, Moritz shouted joyfully"
"Hey my old friend," Vera called out, avoiding eye contact. Moritz sensed it. "Let me help you with your load," he grabbed her luggage and dragged the bags across the tiny terminal. "My name is Boris I am your new cameraman, the other man uttered extending his hand. Vera turned to look at Moritz but he was already a few steps in front. "Welcome aboard," she replied and kept on walking.
They were own by a chartered plane to Kinshasa airport. Whilst midight Vera began to hallucinate. The high altitude and toxic blood made her lightheaded. She became nervous, paranoid, and frightened. She gazed out of the small window of the chartered plane and froze. She saw her older self, transitioning from a baby in the womb to an angry old woman.
The frames zip zapped back and forth, and somehow her hair caught fire. She screamed and found herself in the toilet.
When she came out she was soaked and dripping in blood, she had shaved her hair and cut her wrists.
She walked up and down the aisle greeting ancestors, she had never heard of. The plane was suddenly full of familiar faces, though she could not name them. Her dead kids appeared, they were pillow fighting, shouting, and chasing each other down the hallway. Her husband sat in his favorite chair and drank wine whilst reading a paper. When he saw her, he blew a kiss and continued as if all was normal. She tried to call out their names, the louder she called the more they moved further away. She began shaking violently and screaming uncontrollably. When she opened her eyes Moritz was holding her tight

against her seat.

"What happened?" She asked warily.

"I think you had a nightmare, have some water." Her clothes were damp with sweat. She sipped the water and went into the plane toilet. She locked herself in for a considerable time. When she got out she had shaved her head. She resembled a tomboy and it kind of suited her. Moritz and Boris discreetly exchanged eye contact and kept their thoughts to themselves.

"What happened?" She asked warily.

Chapter 7

When they landed, the day's temperature was beyond survival. It was hot and the sweat created a maze of running running lagoons on people's faces. A lot of foreigners packed the airport, mostly french speaking natives.

As Vera and her crew searched for their host, a huge bearded man crept behind them.

"Hello, bonjour, Bienvenue en république du Congo (welcome to the Democratic Republic of Congo)," he barked.

"Please call me Freddy, and I am both your driver and your everything. He grinned and shook their hands tightly. He was a heavily built man in his fifties, wearing an old green jacket and an open-necked shirt.

"I hope your flight was a pleasant one. We have about six hours to cover to get to Bukavu," he continued as sweat ran down his face.

"Which organization are you working for," Vera asked politely.

"Ah, my apologizes," and he removed his identification card from inside his shirt. She recognized the logo and the official stamp and nodded her head. They were people of all ages wandering around, chatting, and laughing. "You have been to Africa before may I ask."

"Yes, I have been to Cape Town, Harare a couple of times, and Morocco too," Moritz answered.

"Oh, that's paradise. It's a different world here. Um,

before we embark on our journey, there are a few things you must be aware of," he said with an intense look. "There are a lot of gangs out there. You cannot take anyone for granted, young or old. I must say how bad it may sound. In some places, white people are not popular at all. You are all considered to be French or Dutch, and that's a bad thing. If there is anything you would like to do urgently, it's better to do it here in Kinshasa. We don't have so many amenities in Bukavu, I should warn you." Vera and Moritz looked at each other nervously. Soldiers and police officers manned the airport.

Occasionally gunshots could be heard in the distance. As they exited the airport, two other men greeted them and helped with the luggage. There was a second Land Rover with six security personnel. Freddy drove at high speed. His excuse was that they were snipers around the area who killed for fun. They sped past dilapidated buildings and shanty suburbs.

Chapter 8

The vast difference in infrastructure was genuinely shocking. "Congo is known to produce some of the rarest minerals in the world. We have bauxite, diamonds, petroleum, uranium, gold.
You name it. So much wealth, but there is nothing to show for all that." Freddy disclosed.
Vera observed the landscape quietly. She saw war-torn roads and badly damaged houses. Whenever Buses and cars would slow down, groups of women and children ran after them wanting to sell their proceeds. Men moved around aimlessly, and young boys played soccer on the streets.
"Kinshasa is not as bad as they say," Freddy broke the silence. "Not after you have tasted a Primus, Pale lager," he said as he pulled out a pack from underneath his seat. He cracked open one with his teeth and offered
it to Vera, who was sitting in front. She hesitated, she was about to chastise him, and he said, "when you are in Rome, you do what the Romans do," he argued. Vera grabbed the bottle and took a sip. Freddy beamed with delight and laughed. "The best there is. Two more for the gentleman at the back." He opened two more bottles and gave them to Moritz and Boris. From the rearview mirror, he noticed the two helpers staring at him with expressive eyes. "And two more for Gilbert and Moses at the back." Gilbert and Moses grinned in approval since it was rare to drink blended beers. They drank

more of their traditional local homemade brewers.
Freddy was ranting about his time during the war. He bragged that he had downed an enemy helicopter with a pistol. "Being a Tutsi," he elaborated on how he had strangled 15 Hutus with his bare hands to escape from prison. He told them he was a former commander in the Belgians army. He justified his overweight by overeating cassava and drinking a lot of European beer.

They drove out of the city and through a narrow road between tall trees. It began to rain steadily, and Freddy pulled over and covered the Landrover with an overhead tent.
After a few minutes, the sun came out blazing hot.
The clouds were astonishingly white, and the scenery suddenly appeared beautiful. Boris took out a small camera and captured the incredible landscape that disappeared into a valley and surfaced again further ahead. Most of the time, Freddy drove in silence, only erupting briefly if there was a cultural monument or a site of historical remembrance, which he described with much enthusiasm and passion.

"That rock over there, that is where um, 100 000 Tutsis died defending their village, defending their women and of course their cattle. Yes, many children, men, and old women died fighting against the Hutus," he choked and wiped the sweat from his forehead.

Freddy explained passionately about what he knew and what he guessed. They were suddenly disturbed by loud music from the second vehicle. The soldiers were drinking alcohol heavily and were urging their driver to speed up. Their jeep followed too closely behind. They were almost bumper to bumper. Vera sank in her seat and clutched tightly to the door. The driver of the other vehicle was erratic and reckless. He was swerving and hooting, pushing Freddy to go faster. The cars shook and bumped as they unexpectedly encountered potholes and patches of grass in the middle of the road. A moment of confusion was when a half-naked woman emerged from the bush, totally terrified and covered in blood.

She took a glance at them and dashed across the road, disappearing into the thick forest. Freddy swerved to his right and slammed on the brakes as he grabbed his gun. The car driver behind screeched to a halt, and the soldiers swiftly slipped out, ready for an ambush. A volley of gunshots burst out in all directions.

Shadows of little figures scattered, retreating, and melted into the bush. Vera and her crew cowered underneath the seats, visibly shaken and in fear. It was dif cult for them to comprehend what had just transpired. They stared at each other in bewilderment.

Freddy nervously wiped his brow, gasping for air. His eyes menacingly searching for any movements as his grip on the gun tightened.

Finally, he sighed. "There are a lot of small gangs of bandits causing havoc among vulnerable villagers, especially young girls. These scavengers are heartless and have no morals. Most of them are ex-soldiers. They murder innocent civilians and destroy their possessions." Freddy elaborated, shaking his head. They drove along a rugged coastline and through a steep mountainous gorge. The area was mysteriously dangerous as they navigated too close to cliff hangers. There were massive boulders and glimpses of hidden caves. The once drunk soldiers had suddenly become alert. Their gazes and bloodshot eyes gave an eerie warning. The sound of the vehicles was a major giveaway. The road was riddled with blown-up potholes. A convoy of burnt army trucks ripped apart stood silently close to the edge of the precipice. The soldiers had their guns pointed in different directions, ready to fire at any given moment. Their movements and actions anticipated an attack. They came to an area where two substantial rugged mountains lined up with a maze of green trees on both sides.

Freddy was praying as he drove cautiously, avoiding rocks, and deliberately placed long logs of wood. His eyes were like golf balls wide and seemed to rotate. He was looking out for tiny movements and landmines. Vera, Moritz, and Boris became fixated on Freddy's gestures and actions.

"Stay low. This area is dangerous," muffled Freddy. Vera squeezed tightly between the seats. Moritz was scared to death. His spectacles were mist with sweat.

They stayed low, expecting to be shot at or to hear

gunshots buzzing close by. "Hallelujah," puffed Freddy. "We are out of danger. That place scares the hell out of me. We always get attacked when passing through this area. I guess we got lucky today. Maybe they saw you, Vera, and got spooked. It's not every day when you see an angel surrounded by soldiers, especially around these parts of the world. They probably thought they had seen a goddess, "ha ha ha," he belted out laughing, "well you are a goddess," and he pumped up the volume of the radio.

It was almost getting dark when they arrived at the campsite. Freddy hooted three times and flashed his headlights. A guard rail went up, and soldiers with AK47 suspiciously peeped into the jeeps as they drove by. There was nothing that resembled a refugee camp. A few scattered huts built on top of small hills and a large thatched house stood in the middle. Metal signs of the United Nations and UNESCO swung from a tree. Soldier's tents and a few broken vehicles lay between trees and a barricade of sacks filled with sand. As the car came to a halt, a few pale faces observed them silently.

Their presence had stimulated some form of interest among therefugees as they grinned and excitedly jostled to catch a glimpse of the new arrivals.

"I guess you all have jet lag. I will show you your villas. The chef will feed you with our local delicacies," Freddy bantered them. They got out, stretching their cramped limbs. Vera and her crew were puzzled by the sight of the camp. It was as if they were on a different planet. The monotonous hum of the generator deafened the place.

"This side is the suburbs. Over there lies the real camp,

directly beneath the hills," Freddy yelled, pointing to a sizeable endless surface of white and blue tents. He took out a packet of cigarettes and passed it around. "Welcome to Bukavu Camp, madam, here; you will find great news and interesting coverage for your customers. Come on, let the cameras roll." He burst out laughing as he led them to their new homes.

Bukavu is a city in the eastern part of the Republic of Congo, tucked at Rwanda's edge. It used to be constantly under attack until the rebels were driven across the border.

Vera stood in the middle of her new home, a hidden cluster of round huts neatly cleaned up for foreign dignitaries. There were a single bed and a tiny table next to a clothing stand.

On the wall, a small mirror attached to a piece of string dangled above the table. An odor of an old burnt fragrance circulated in the air.

Vera heaved and dumped herself on the mattress, causing the springs to squeak, sagging the bed to the floor. She shrieked and struggled to get up.

At the back of the hut was a shared shower, and a distance away, a pit latrine stood isolated from everything else.

„Not what you expected huh, they could have warned us about the non-existence of five-star hotels," Moritz chatted as he knocked on the wooden frame.

„I have been to too many places, but this is something else. You have to watch every step you make constantly."

„Not only that, you got to watch your back too. So, when do we start."

"There is never a perfect time to start. A reporter is always on the job 24hrs a day."

"I will be right next door; when you feel a twitch scream,
I will come running."
"I am sure the guards outside are up to the task."
"Well, then see you in the morning, and don't let the bed
bugs bite," he gulped his beer and disappeared into the
darkness.

Chapter 9

That night Vera had a recurring dream. She had flashbacks of her family. She saw them walking along a path on a camping trip. And as they reached a certain point, they were mysteriously led into an alien world. The exact sequence played out the whole night. The next day when sVera woke up, it was almost midday. She had underestimated her tiredness.

Outside, a crowd of soldiers and social workers were in a feeding frenzy. They had metal plates of food, shouting and screaming, as they ran up and down in different directions.

Moritz and Boris sat on white plastic chairs under a tent, watching the commotion. Boris was taking photographs and cleaning up his camera lenses. Moritz had his laptop on his lap designing assignments. They had no clue about where and how to start. Vera strolled towards them with a big smile on her face.

"Gentlemen, are you ready for our mission? Because if you are not, then that's too bad." They cast their eyes on her and wondered what she was about to say.

"One of the social workers told me there is a white building not far from here, where most child soldiers hang out. We could start from there. I mean, these are the kids who have been in the midst of it all."

"That's an excellent idea, I am sure they have a lot to tell," Boris said getting up. Moritz nodded his head in agreement.
"We will have an escort for our safety, and we should pack some water and candies." Vera felt as if a huge rock had been removed from her back. Her bald head glittered, and her face radiated. She looked relaxed, and her spirit hovered above her head. Her mind was free, and she felt her body regenerated. The comforting weather and the unpleasant environment seriously contradicted each other.
They had a few discussions with the head of security and were allowed to move around freely. Vera led as if she belonged there. She was a woman who had a lot to prove, and her chances were very slim. The blitz of fresh air combined with a stench from the camp breezed past the ozone layer and spread in different directions. It was what it is, and she felt great. That feeling was soon wiped off after only a few steps. She found herself surrounded by tiny figures with sorrowful eyes. She was overcome with grief and confronted by guilt. When she looked around, she saw extreme poverty and
desperation on people's faces. Almost half of the refugees had a limb missing. Men, women, and children stood, sat, lay helplessly on the ground. The gazes of the babies were deep and worrisome.
Boris, with sweat dripping, snapped pictures and gave out candies as they went by.
"Do you people want me to lose my job? You cannot go anywhere without me," Freddy barked from behind. „I was searching for you everywhere. O."

"Oh, Freddy, great to see you. We thought you were

busy," Vera answered politely.

"And we have a guard with us," Moritz intervened. Freddy sulked, „If there is gunfire, you think he will stand and protect you." He shook his head and gave them a lecture about Bukavu.

"This camp is a disgrace to our ancestors. Bukavu belonged to the Bushi Kingdom. Chief Muluzi governed it. Muluzi means nobility. They were noble, rich, and educated before the Arabs and Europeans arrived. Bukavu was a paradise on earth; as you can see, waterfalls surround it. It's built on five peninsulas, evergreen grass, scenic locations you can only dream about. Look at the hills. You can climb up and get lost forever. There are sacred areas not to be messed with, or else you will disappear for good. The war between the Hutus and Tutsis has turned this once paradise of Africa into a

poverty-stricken hub. Our ancestors will never forgive us for turning our backs on them. They are angry, and we deserve to be punished."

Freddy was emotional and passionate; his facial expressions twitched and tensed as he spoke. Vera, Moritz, and Boris stood in attention and listened earnestly. „The first thing you do, wherever you go, is to learn about the cultural history of that place. If you don't, the chances of upsetting the local chiefs are high. You need to be aware of the different cultures around here. Don't take things lightly.

The masses are hungry; they are desperate, but what you should know is, no matter how much help you offer them, they will always resent colonialists."

"No one is a colonialist among us, and we are here to expose to the world the atrocities of the war, using children as soldiers, that is nefarious," Moritz replied, feeling

agitated. Freddy abruptly turned towards him, scoffed, and scorned.

"Your knowledge and wisdom about your culture are quite impressive, Messieur Freddy," Vera graciously praised him.

The remark caught him unaware. He twitched, and his eyes paced the ground glowing with pride. Boris rubbed his anger in his ear while staring at Vera. „There is an abundance of hidden wealth and plenty of history to be learned. It will be a great pleasure if you could find time to show us the beauty of Bukavu and share with us and the whole world your great

knowledge," Vera praised him.

"On camera, of course," Boris added. Freddy could not hide his emotions.

"You want me to be on television, O boy, I will tell you the deepest secrets of this nation." He looked up to the heavens and glorified God. „Let your name be exalted, O Lord. I feel your blessings and kindness, your love and your mercy Lord.

Thank you, Jesus, thank you, Lord." Boris filmed him as he prayed.

Freddy took them to an area where most child soldiers were housed for rehabilitation. Some seemed too young and thin to be able to carry a rifle. Others, although still in their youth, had chiseled bodies. The one thing they had in common was the cold stare in their eyes. It was deep, bloodshot, and fearless. Freddy gathered them together and explained the purpose of Vera and her crew's visit. They mumbled in Kinyarwanda, which is their local language. Boris startled them when he flashed his camera, causing them to disperse.

"Listen, guys, please stop. We only want to hear about your experiences. We want to know what you saw?

What you went through? I understand you went through terrible situations, but if you don't tell us, we will never know."

Vera pulled out a box of chocolates and biscuits. „I brought something for you guys."

The kids immediately stopped and slowly walked towards her.

They each hungrily snatched the snacks from her and turned around, muttering and gibbering. A cloud of dust swirled nearby, and a mist-like air whizzed past.

Vera was puzzled by the sudden change of weather. When the air had cleared, the kids were busy munching their gifts.

A young boy stood out among them. He was light skinned with big ears and a pointed nose next to thick lips. He stood motionless, looking at her innocently. His big eyes and deep gaze concealed his thoughts. He was thin, tall, with a conspicuous Adam's apple. Vera wondered if he had reached adolescence yet. She walked over to him with a smile and a chocolate bar in her hand. She stood in front of him without saying a word. He stared back at her and tilted his head, and chirped.

"My name is Kojo." His sunny smile revealed white spaced teeth. „They say chocolates are bad for your teeth. I don't have teeth, and I don't believe these soft, delicious cookies can rot my teeth. I can remove a buck of a tree with my mouth."

He grinned like a Cheshire cat, emitting fumes of a yellowish cloud. „You are far away from home, yet you are home. Your anguish, your suffering has brought you back. The ancestors welcome you, Vera."

As he spoke those words, Vera felt her blood shooting to the brain. There was a sudden rush of goosebumps developing from her feet to her neck. Her nerves protruded, and her heart turbocharged, pumping vigorously. Hair grew out of her bald head. She became pale and weak. The sound of his deep, soothing voice pierced through her head and traveled all over her body. His voice was of a man, but his body was of a boy.

His lips twitched as his words flowed out smoothly. "The spirit of a mother knows no boundaries. In death, in life, it tears through souls and eliminates the invisible for the love of one." His was poetic and hypnotizing. "Nothing wretches the heart more than the occurrence of a mystifying dream." He smiled childishly before snatching the chocolate bar and disappeared into the crowd.
A scruffy-looking young boy was hiding behind a tree observing Kojo, with extreme anger in his eyes. When he saw the yellowish steam coming out of Kojo's mouth, he cross-eyed his eyes and vanished into thin air.

"You look like you have seen a ghost. Are you all alright? Oh jeez, you went pale," Boris looked at her, worried. She did not say a word. She turned around and slowly walked back to her room.
The three men stood astonished, wondering what had

happened to her. Boris wanted to run after her, but Freddy stopped him.
"She must have lost a child. She is still having pain. Let her rest for the day. You guys can get the job done, right," Boris and Moritz hesitantly agreed.

Chapter 10

The scruff young boy emerged among a clan of immortal beings and transformed into a tall muscled Monko warrior. He had long dreadlocked hair, and his body armor was of shiny tungsten. Above his thick nose and big lips, a pair of owl round brownish eyes hid in a bulging forehead. He carried a diamond spear as heavy as iron-coated lead. His given name was Aragognto Paradza, which meant to seek and destroy. Giants of Monko immortal beings swayed encased in similar attire.

The elders adorned different types of animal skins and spiritual garments.

The immeasurable spiritual realm was built inside Mount Kilimanjaro. Millions of grappling immortal beings wandered angrily in circles, searching for vengeance. Aragognto Paradza breezed past them, sometimes making himself invisible as he headed for the realm's Begamu chamber. The immortal beings had supernatural powers beyond any human capabilities.

They were telekinetic and had the ingenuity to move objects using only the power of the mind. They could teleport themselves and their belongings around the continent. Although combat-ready and well skilled, as spiritual beings, they could not engage physically in any battles.

They had to endure watching their descendants suffer in their land. The immortal beings and the water spirits lived happily side-by-side as the African continent's sole guardians until the invaders penetrated them.
The immortal beings accused the water spirits of granting passage to enemies who had masqueraded as merchants into their world. There was friction between the two forces, which was further fueled by the birth of Kojo. A child of a female human and a merman.
When the enemies launched an invasion, many African Kingdoms and their people escaped to the mountains. They were harbored and protected by the immortals' Gods and later on turned into ancestral spiritual beings. However, not all immortal beings agreed with the notion that the water spirits were sellouts.

Therefore some allied with the water spirits and were granted access into their world. The immortal beings spread across Africa, establishing permanent bases and fortresses in sacred mountains, caves, and forests.
Various mortal beings established a spiritual communication link between them and their many tribes. The immortal beings could move around and live freely among different cultures and sometimes would make their presence felt but stayed out of sight of the mortal beings. Aragognto Paradza stood outside an inconspicuous, heavily built cloud vault. There were heads of lions, buffalos, elephants, and zebras stuck by the entrance. Only an elder with stronger powers could allow you through by taking control of your mind.

Chief Kandagu and Mbuya Hanevi sat on floating shrines. They were emblems of royalty and other ornaments meticulously displayed all over the dominion. As soon as his spirit was granted permission to enter, he immediately became possessed by a higher spiritual power that took control of his spiritual powers. Aragognto Paradza's spirit levitated towards them and froze in the middle of smoking shadows. More invisible spiritual homo sapiens started revealing themselves around him. Their pale faces were painted with black and white marks.

There was no exchange of words. Everything was done telepathically. You could only tell there was a conversation in progress through the head movements.

Aragognto Paradza attested to them that he had finally found the bloodline's descendant responsible for the massacres and betrayal of their people. They needed her blood to reverse the curse they had thrust upon themselves.

He proclaimed he had seen Kojo in liaison with her, which meant he might be trying to show favor in return for being accepted back by the water spirits. There was a commotion among them as the regalia began to shake. They disagreed about whether she was

the authentic bloodline, as they only had one shot. Aragognto Paradza recited about the yellowish smoke that had emitted from Kojo's nose. The place became still. The spiritual walls grunted and yammered, releasing thick dark clouds of smoke.

Eerie whispers echoed, and flames of fire flickered in multiple spots. Suddenly there were quick soft strokes of drumbeats permeating throughout the enclave.

Chief Kandagu and Mbuya Hanevi zoned in and silenced them. Aragognto Paradza had to convey the message to the mortal beings.

A ritual had to be carried out in a sacred cave,with a virgin pool of water and an endless bottom. Vera's blood had to be sacrificed to appease the superior guardians of the spiritual world. Before Aragognto Paradza was released, Mbuya Hanevi took his spirit on tour. She transformed into a middle-aged woman.
Her face was smooth and shiny; her voice was soft, clear, but filled with anger.
"Our spiritual guided beacon is in disarray. The spiritual souls of our people have become too scattered. The bond has been weakened and scattered seeds weaken the bond. The strength of the African continent is a spiritual magnetic ball, that feeds on each and every individual. When one disconnects, its powers decrease. Masses have migrated, and many more will befall ill, thrust upon us by those who seek what we possess. A happy soul stays home, and a sad soul goes astray. If you seek to destroy, sow chaos, create a remedy, a desperate person will fall for anything." She walked with a measured pace in the middle of the clouds as she spoke to him, still in levitation, surrounded by green fields.
"We might have lost the battle but not our continent. The time has come to awaken the sleeping giants." Her face changed shades as she spoke.

Chapter 11

Later that evening, Vera was troubled. She was in deep thoughts. Kojo's words had touched her in a way that she could not interpret. She lay on her back, her mind racing, and in tatters.

"You are far away from home, yet you are home. Your anguish, your suffering has brought you back. The ancestors welcome you, Vera." The words were vivid in her head. "He knew my name," she murmured. "Nothing wretches the heart more than the occurrence of a mystifying dream."

"He knew I had dreamt of my family." She was concerned but eager to nd out more.

The following day, she seemed to have recovered from the trauma. There was something outlandish about her. Her hair had grown almost to her shoulders. She found Moritz and Boris in a secret discussion.

When they noticed her, they pretended to be busy with their gadgets. "I have found one," a loud voice echoed. It was Freddy approaching with a young tad in tow. He was beaming with delight.

"This young man is called Kojo. He has lived more lives than any of us."

"How do you know that? Good guess." Kojo said, giggling awkwardly. They created space for him to sit and made him feel comfortable. Boris secretly positioned his camera, afraid of making him nervous. "Kojo was rescued by the UN army the same day you arrived. He was abducted when he was only eight years old and spend almost ve years with the rebel army. Vera forced a smile and held his cracked hands with her eyes closed. She was expecting the same evolution to take place, but nothing happened. Moritz and Boris exchanged suspicious glances. They were concerned by her attitude. She stepped back and sat quietly, observing Kojo. After a moment of unpleasant silence, Moritz pushed a plate full of cookies towards him. He grinned and whistled, enjoying the food platter.

"What can you tell us, Mr? Do you remember anything? About how you got kidnapped?" Moritz asked politely. Freddy opened a bottle of Fanta and gave it to him. He gulped the whole bottle, burped, and burped. "Sorry." His wandering, small eyes gave him away. He pinched a few more cookies from the plate and sped off laughing.

"I suspect these kids are high on some weird drug."

"Drugs!" Vera exclaimed.

"You mean there is cocaine in the camp." Boris pondered.

"No, not cocaine, other types of drugs. Ganja, glue, benzine, anything to blast you off. The camp is full of shenanigans. If you want to get high, you can always nd something to take you home. Forgive me about the naughty kid; I guess he just wanted food. He is the one who came up to me, and I have never seen him before."

"Well, I don't think we should be bribing or forcing anyone to divulge their past skirmishes. Most seem to have questionable cognitive abilities." Boris asserted. Vera got up and went to look for Kojo.

"I need a moment, I will loiter around a bit, by myself."
"You might need to take some chocolates with you," Boris
called after her.
She had no idea where to start searching for him. She
wandered until she noticed a group of four older people
observing her from a distance. They had old rags thrown
over their shoulders. Their stares made her shiver. She
reluctantly steered herself towards them.
A bird squeal distracted her attention brie y, as she got her
focus back, she realized they had melted into thin air. In
annoyance, she let out some obscenities. "Shit! Dick head.
Where the hell did they go to?" Daydreaming with her head
firmly focused on the ground, she found herself walking quite
a distance before she detected she had taken a wrong turn.
She scratched her head, thinking. "How did that happen? I
only walked a short distance." She looked around, and the
camp was no longer in sight. She found herself in a forest
and had no idea how she got there.
"This is weird, really weird."
"Hello, hello Vera, Vera." She was startled, and happy
someone had recognized her. The voice sounded familiar; she
turned and saw Kojo sitting on a rock. Still mystified, she
slowly walked towards him.
"You must have taken the wrong turn. No one hardly comes
here. Have you brought me some of those nice cookies?"
Vera was still in confusion. "My mind was preoccupied. I
didn't realize I went off track. It's weird; I have no idea how I
got here."
"You should learn to listen to your inner voice. It's
beautiful and peaceful here. You like it?" She twisted her
lips, searching for what to say. "Yes, it is! Why are you
here alone?" She found the courage to ask.
"I am not alone." Vera looked around but could not see
anyone else. "Well, I don't see anyone except you."
He glared at her, which made her nervous.

"I got a Crunch bar for you." His eyes glowed.

"I love chocolates, and you have a pure heart."

"Thank you," Vera answered. There was a moment of silence as Kojo devoured the chocolate bar.

"How do you nd the camp?" She asked curiously. "Nobody should be living in a camp. Nobody should be a refugee in their land. People are in cages like slaves." He spoke without hesitation.

"How long were you in the army?"

He sighed and kept on munching his chocolate. "As long as I can remember. This continent is the pillar of the universe. The soil you are standing on is the blood spilled by your forefathers." Vera was stunned.

"Our spiritually guided beacon is in disarray. The spiritual souls of our people have become too scattered. The bond has been weakened, and scattered seeds weaken the bond. The strength of the African continent is a spiritual magnetic ball that feeds on every individual. When one disconnects, its power decreases. Masses have migrated, enslaved, and many more will befall ill, thrust upon us by those who seek what we possess. A happy soul stays home, and a sad soul goes astray. If you seek to destroy, sow chaos, create a remedy, a desperate soul will fall for anything. We might have lost the battle but not our continent. The time has come to awaken the sleeping giants." He spoke coolly, with authority as his face changed shades. Vera dwelled in his soulful voice that momentarily spellbound her.

"Do you have any family?" He looked at her and shook his head. Tears started streaming down his cheeks.

"Were you mistreated in any way?"

He put half of the chocolate bar in his pocket and stared ahead of him.

"What do you see when you look around?" he asked her with a firm voice. She lifted her head and focused on her surroundings. The scenery had transformed. She surveyed the area without blinking. Her eyes grew wider. She was alarmed at what lay in front of them. What looked like green plantations were, in reality, fields of graves. She choked.

"Who are these people?"

"Good question; I thought you knew."

"Me? How am I supposed to know?"

"You are the chosen one."

"Excuse me? Before she could say anything, He let out an eerie cry. "I can tell you a thousand stories about any of these graves." He sprang up and gestured to her to follow him. Vera jerked as she was about to get up; a giant sinister shadow hovered above her. She froze. A swift breeze blew her hair over her face. She shrieked, stumbled, and nervously turned around, but there was nothing sinister to be seen.

Kojo kept on walking, unfazed. She got up and dashed after him. For the first time, she noticed he was carrying an AK 47 on his back. "Why does he have a gun?" She whispered to herself. "Because I am a soldier," he yelled. She paused, scratching her head. "I did not say that aloud."

"Stuki lies here," he shouted and began to narrate, standing next to a hump of soil. "He was a family man who was loved by many. The chief got him strangled because he refused to give up his wife. After his death, the chief married his wife and his three daughters. Yes, the chief made them his wives."

He looked across the graveyard and grinned. "Uh, there he is, Callisto. He was a giant of a warrior, and he got mauled to death.

They put him in a cage with two lions, the reason being;

he had fallen in love with the chief's daughter." He stood by the grave for a while as if reminiscing. Vera listened attentively, secretly recording him.

"Here lies a family of ve. They were burnt alive after being accused of witchcraft. Because a child tripped and fell in front of their house and broke his leg."

He strode, calling each grave by name. Vera followed him as if she was a little child scared of the dark. The whole time she had a feeling, the spirits of the occupants of the graves were lurking in her shadow. Kojo was mumbling, zig-zagging through the graveyard. A white cloud of dust emanated from beyond the trees and blanketed the burial ground. Vera, in a state of shock, fell to her knees.

"A lot of potholes in this area. Are you ok?" Freddy uttered.

She remained on her knees, feeling confused and embarrassed.

"Let me help you up."

"I am fine," she got up and dusted herself. To her surprise, she was back in the camp. She searched around suspiciously as the three men stared at her speechlessly and in astonishment.

"You didn't hurt, yourself did you?" Moritz asked her. She shook her head, disoriented.

"Nope," she replied, unsure of what had just transpired. Boris and Moritz observed her from the car, wondering if she was drunk. She remembered her tape recorder.

"Guys, I want you to listen to this, I know it sounds crazy, but a few minutes ago, I was in the middle of a cemetery with Kojo.

He told me some fascinating stories, and I have them tape." She pulled out the recorder and pressed play.

"Umm, there he is, Callisto! He was a giant of a warrior; he got mauled to death. They put him in a cage with two lions because he had fallen in love with the chief's daughter."
"You see, I told you." They looked at her befuddled. "What's going on Vera, should we take you to the hospital?" Moritz

spoke, feeling concerned.
"I just told you what happened a couple of minutes ago, and she pressed play again.
"Here lies a family of ve. They burnt them alive after being accused of witchcraft."
"You see, it's all on tape." She repeated her words. "Vera, the tape is empty. There is nothing there," Boris responded, feeling annoyed. She wanted to argue, but there was no point.
She thought she was going mad. Only she could hear Kojo's voice.
"Why don't you come with me and see the beauty of Bukavu," Freddy shouted, distracting their attention.

Chapter 12

It was early in the morning, and the villagers had already gathered outside Chief Chirau's compound. He was a respected and feared spiritual leader of his district. There were a lot of cases to be judged that day. He sat with a group of advisers around are sniffling snuff. His nephew, who worked as his herdboy, had eloped with the wife of another village chief. They were trying to figure out how to settle the dispute without shedding any blood. From nowhere, a violent gust of wind swirled in a nearby field.

It uprooted maize plants and anything in its way. Chief Chirau and his men stared in disbelief. It grew bigger and shot up, turning into a whirlwind.
"Go and get the drums, quick. Women start ululating," yelled Chief Chirau.
There was confusion as men ran to get the drums, and the women gathered dancing and ululating. â€œDonâ€™t forget the beer,â€ he screamed. Chief Chirau sniffed some more snuff and threw some to the ground. He grabbed a mug of brewed beer and gulped it. He looked nervous, and sweat rained on his bloodshot eyes. The whirlwind gathered its pace and raced towards them. By now, a fully dressed up team of dancers was jumping up and down worshipping the ancestors.
The drumbeats swelled into the atmosphere and echoed

far and wide. As the whirlwind was about to swallow the whole crowd, it just miraculously died down and melted into the air.

In a fit, Chief Chirau wrenched, and his body was dragged and lifted off the ground. He shook and grunted. The villagers upped their performances; the women knelt, clapping their hands, praising, and asking for forgiveness. Chief Chirau dropped to the ground; he lay quivering and rumbling. Four strong men held him down, afraid he might hurt himself.

A group of natives came running from nearby homesteads. They had drums and matching traditional clothing. When they appeared, the crowd erupted in celebration. They beat the drums with passion and a spiritual frenzy. Older men and women snuffed and got drunk from locally brewed beer.

A young lady freaked out and began to shake violently and uncontrollably.

She pushed everyone out of the way and growled like a lion.

She spoke in a strange inaudible older man's voice. "She is here, the bloodline of the cursed, the one from across the seas. She is in the camp. She must be sacrificed, Veraa, Veraaa, Veraaa. In a bottomless virgin pool, inside a sacred cave, her blood must be spilled, or else there will be no rain, your animals will die, your children will become sick, Veraa, Veraa." The voice was hoarse and uneven. Only a few spiritually gifted understood what she said.

After those words, the young lady fell to the ground. Chief Chirau overpowered the four men and roared, sending shivers into the crowd.

He grabbed his spear and started running towards the camp. Village warriors joined him, running through the forest and across charred woodlands. They ran as if they were being chased by hyenas under the spell of Aragognto Paradza.

Vera got into the jeep, glassy-eyed and deranged. Freddy drove a short distance through a maze of tents and awkward structures. He halted outside a fenced area with a huge white and yellow tent anchored in the middle. There wasn't much activity going on. A handful of people were lying around in the dirt under makeshift plastic shelters. They went through the controlled gate and walked towards the tent. The place had a mysterious feeling. Death was close by. There were a monotonous buzz and disgusting odor. It soon became clear the buzzing came from flies, feeding on open wounds. The trio halted and reconsidered.

The sight of two women lying on the ground partially covered by grass shocked them. Both of them had their four limbs missing. The women stared at them, their eyes full of contempt.

"Come on, keep moving," Freddy pressed them on. It was a heart-wrenching glimpse. Their wounds were not correctly bandaged, and they cried in pain, pleading for mercy. They continued walking, casting doubtful peeks in different directions.

When Freddy pulled the plastic blind of the tent open, Vera froze.

"You wanted a story, be my guest." He smirked.

The place was full of badly injured souls. She saw one

doctor and two nurses in charge of over a thousand moaning patients. It was hell on earth. Freddy looked at his guests sarcastically.

"Does the outside world care about ethnic cleansing? Those hoodlums you were feeding are responsible for these acts.

They carry a guilty conscience regardless of them being brainwashed and fed with narcotics. Those babyfaced goons can turn into savages in a split second. Their souls belong to the devil. They have participated in too many primitive, horrendous attacks. Their souls can never be saved." Freddy was full of hatred as he spoke. "We need to run a report, Vera. Should I prepare talking points?"

Although Moritz was sickened, he saw an opportunity playing in realtime in front of his eyes. No matter how heinous the situation was, this would make great news worldwide, and Freddy wanted to be on television.

As Vera surged forward, she noticed a woman who had suffered a fourth-degree burn. She lost control of the situation. Her head began to spin, and she became nauseated. Her mind flooded with flashbacks of her family burning in the house.

Their screams and cries for help swarmed her ears. She backtracked and bolted out of the building. Moritz ran a couple of steps after her. She was too quick for him. He stood outside in deep thoughts. "Vera is losing it, but we need to do our job. We can work on voiceovers later."

He told Boris and instructed him to lm and capture as many shots as he could.

Vera kept on running and sobbing. She was in a state

of mental confusion. The soldiers and refugees thought she was getting mad, and they laughed at her. She ran deep into the woods until she stumbled and fell, with tears in her eyes. The recurrence of the painful death of her family had overwhelmed her. It left her grief-stricken and heartbroken.

Memories of her family muddled her mind, and she painfully sobbed. In the midst of it all, something caught her eye.

She was startled when she faintly caught a glimpse of a familiar face watching her. She stiffened while wiping her eyes to get a better look. The figure disappeared unnaturally. In her mind, she thought she had seen the man with a leather jacket, who had provoked her on the plane, while she was on her way to Munich.

A strange cry incited the trees; they started swaying and hissing rhythmically. Her head was about to blow up; she thought she was getting crazy. The whole place was moving as if in space. Unfamiliar faces, eyes, and scary cries popped in and out. She crunched, holding her ears. Mysterious creatures were observing her. She remained in that position for a long time, and when she thought she had regained her composure, she straightened up. A ball of thick grey mist jiggled in front of her. Her mind was all over the place. She got up and tried to run, but the fog ballooned, moving stealthily, swallowing everything in its way. The whole forest became engulfed and obscured as if a godly creature was roaming the streets. Susurrus murmurings reverberated around her, and she was scared stiff. Twigs snapped, and windblown leaves crackled, echoing in the distance. In confusion, she thought Moritz was

searching for her. "Veraaaaa, Veraaaaaaaa, Veraaaa."

Her name echoed. She suspiciously listened to the tone.
Only to realize the voice was coming from within
herself. The mist naturally turned into a colorful thick
fog. She peered forward with the cautiousness of a
blind man. "Hello, hello, can anybody hear me? Please
help me?" She slowly babystepped, venturing deeper
into the woods. The ominous sound of humming and
whirring rose and dropped multiple times. It sounded
more like a spiritual frenzy party. She was terrified, she
became numb and dropped to her knees, coiling
herself into a ball. It began to rain; the mist and the fog
evaporated into thin air.

There was a strong gust of wind that brought freezing
temperatures. The grass turned into glass. She shivered
and trembled. Like a miracle, out popped the sun from
beneath the clouds, and paradise was born. Birds
chirped, and the sun smiled. The scenery was gorgeous.
There was a clear blue waterfall, thick green bushes,
and steep plain gorges. There were rolls of well-clipped
low lying rounded hills stretching up to the horizon. The
view was breathtaking. Vera got up as if nothing had
happened. She smiled and marveled at the sightings.
She was warm and full of joy. Then it hit her,
"where am I?" She asked herself.

Her eyes scanned the bushes, and somehow it had
become eerie quiet. Somebody had turned off the
music. Nothing moved, nothing breathed. The sudden
transition boggled her.

She turned to her right side, trying to nd a way out. It
was full of gorges and mountains. On the other side,
giant, closely trussed trees intertwined. She stood still,
her life in God's hands.

Chapter 14

Chief Chirau and his warriors hid behind a thick bush on the outskirts of the camp. They had traveled at least eighty kilometers within an hour and the old man still looked and full of energy. He sniffed his snuff and mumbled a few words.

Aragognot Paradza allowed him to use his spiritual eyes. Chief Chirau saw Vera getting into a jeep, he saw her in the makeshift hospital and running out crying. Her whereabouts were shown until she entered the spiritual realm of a well guarded immortal tribe. At that point, his vision was aggressively obscured.

Chapter 15

A tiny sliver of lights sprinkled through the closely knit trees. Silhouetting shadows swayed randomly, giving her shivers. Vera decided to follow the route with gorges and mountains, as it was an open landscape.

She took a single step, and hell broke loose. A loud drumbeat shook the earth, and the gorges and the mountains started to vanish in front of her. A series of scary transitions occurred, a plantation of monstrous trees sprouted, wild animals growled in fighting spirit. Strange aggressive birds chased one another, screams of joy, and kids playing in the water attracted her attention. She was both astonished and paralyzed with fear. Her head began to spin as if she was in a trance.

She was disoriented, hallucinating, and had no sense of direction.

"Jumbo Vera," a voice pierced through her veins and made her blood freeze. An attempt to piss in her pants failed. The tone was out of this world, indescribable. She was ash-frozen and remained still for what seemed like a century, afraid to turn and face the spine-chilling intruder.

"You are most welcome to our world. It wasn't by chance, don't be afraid. We chose you." Vera could feel her ears roasting, her fingernails dropping off one at a time. The voice was gentle, soothing, and harmonious. The sun above her rose gently, and the rainbow silhouettes spread across the sky. Her teardrops softened her cheeks, and she realized she was still alive.

"Why me?" She murmured, and it became caliginous. "In the dark, every shadow is mysterious," his voice drifted into thin air. This time the sun came out blazing and bounced on his chest, silhouetting his face. "Your ancestors broke their word, and you are the sacrifice." He stated.

"Sacrifice, my ancestor, where am I?"

"You are in a spiritual realm, a world far from yours."

"What, spiritual realm?"

"Look again; it's all plain to see."

She hesitantly complied, moving her head slightly from side to side. She repeated the same rhythm a couple of times, but nothing seemed awkward. Before she could say anything, it began to pour heavily. She lurched; within a split second, it started to snow. There was an avalanche of snow falling rapidly from a dry mountainside. The trees swayed synchronical, whooshing and swooshing.

"What did you see, Vera?" It was suddenly calm again. The sun shone brightly and a cool breeze swept by. She gasped and turned her head, expecting to see a godly creature. There was no one except a clear desert with dunes. The upheaval confused her. "Am I getting mad? What's going on with me."

She mumbled, leaning forward with her hands on her knees. Her breath became constricted; she was almost suffocating. "Can you see me?"

She fell back, panic-stricken and dazed.

"Use your spiritual eyes. Open your spiritual eyes."
The words sounded familiar. With a feeling of déjà
vu. She remembered her aunty saying the exact
words when she picked her up from the cafe.
She staggered up and positioned herself for better
judgment. She could only see a desert with dunes.
"Copious in resemblance, obstinate, so was Harald."
Vera's eyes bulged out. The name rang a bell. The
family tree that was once on the wall of her father's
house stated:

Harald Bars born 1610-1710
Harald Bars born 1710-1810
Harald Bars born 1810 1910
Robert Bars born 1910-2010

They were her great grandfathers; she wondered
why they were all named Harald. Great warriors
during their time, her father once said. "No, they
weren't great warriors," came the voice. "Take a
walk with me."
Vera goose-stepped after him, sizzling with a blast of
energy.
She zapped as the ow of electricity rippled through
her veins. A handsome young man appeared before
her. His eyes radiated a yellowish-green twilight. He
was clean-shaven and had small round ears. A green
adinkra covered his body.
(spiritual leaders and other elites wore adinkra
clothes to special occasions,)
"No need to be afraid." His lips did not move as he

spoke. His feet glided through the air as he moved towards a glimmering waterfall. Vera dragged herself behind him. What spooked her the most was his trans-po-
sing face. She felt the energy backtracking and pushing
her deeper into the unknown. She felt mysterious eyes
fixated on her demeanor. She sensed danger around
her. The more they walked into the bush, the darker
it became.
The glimmering waterfall kept changing positions. The
tall trees had thick branches and broad leaves, which
did not permit much sunlight through.
"My name is Sairas," he spoke and went silent.

They came to what looked like a shrine. There were
two huge rocks carved into pyramid-like sculptures. In
front of them were ve separate pools of water, being
fed by a low-level waterfall. The waterfall had different
types of well-polished colorful rocks staked on top of
each other. A variety of unknown exotic owers and
perplexing multicolored thick bushes surrounded the
fountainhead. Shiny gold bars and blinking marbles
covered the floor of the pools. Vera was in awe. The
place was genuinely magnificent. For a moment, she
wished she could live there forever.

"No, you cannot," Sairas interrupted her thoughts.
"Your ancestor committed a heinous crime. And as long
as we exist, his bloodline shall forever be condemned.
In 1610 Harald ventured into our kingdom. He was
found unconscious after his ship had capsized, killing
most of his men. Our Queen, Mama Wata saved him
and kept him alive."
When the name Mama Wata, was mentioned, the trees

shook and whispered. Human-like faces swelled out of the trees and receded in a fury.

There was an aggressive splashing and bubbling in the water.

Sounds of cackling and growling echoed, deafening the forest. Hundreds of small fires popped up around them. Vera knew they were not alone. She felt as if she was in a court of law.

When she turned to face Sairas he had levitated and was swirling in the air. There was complete stillness. His eyes had turned pale red, yet his face remained composed. Vera wished the dream would soon end. She stood next to one of the sculptures with her head bowed, afraid to depart from life.

"Queen Mama Wata became fond of him. She trusted him. After all, he was the first of his kind she had ever encountered.

In the beginning, she thought it was an albino tuna. She brought him into our kingdom and showed him some of our most sacred secrets. For ve hundred years, we have been honoring

and laying our Queen to rest. The sins of your forefathers were thrust upon you. We hold you responsible for our Queen's death. Our retribution will be inflicted on your bloodline until you cease to exist." Vera listened in horror.

"Follow me, bear witness to our hidden world, before you depart. This time no one will ever know." Sairas glided towards the waterfall with Vera behind him. "Your eyes shall

be our eyes in the world to come."

As they got closer to the pools, Vera shook like a leaf when the colorful rocks and bushes began to dismantle and disperse.

She suddenly realized the rocks and the bushes were piles of mermaids and mermen. They were half human and half fish. Like human beings, they came in different forms and sizes. Vera saw giants, short, fat, thin, and tall water spirits.

It was a mixture of beauty and hideous among the many. Most of the mermen straightened up and cast a mean look at her.

Their large fins swayed, shining and glimmering, magnifying the clear, glassy water.

The vast area around them unraveled, revealing millions of square meters of endless seawater. Vera, bone-chilled crumbled, as marine plants submerged and mermen somersaulted.

Sairas pinched her nose and sealed her mouth. He aggressively grabbed her by the leg and dragged her down. The mermaids and mermen screeched and hummed, racing towards the ocean floor like marine ants. They were moving so fast, two blinks and a hundred would have gone by. As soon as they touched the ocean floor, they mysteriously vanished. Vera, drowning and in shock, fought against the bubbles.

Sarais got annoyed, stopped, and held her by the neck with an angrier look. She obliged, and they descended into the abyss disillusioned and hopeless. When they got closer to the ocean floor, Vera closed her eyes, expecting a hard impact, but they just dissolved into the layer beneath.

The mermaids had created an artificial bottom and

built a massive kingdom, the size of an ocean under it. It was a complex of dazzling, flamboyant edifices. Vera burbled like a baby sh in shock. Sarais held his palm close to her chest, and she coughed.

"What is going on? What happened to me? Where am I? Why am I talking underwater?" She freaked out. She was in deep water facing peril. A group of amused spectators had gathered around them and were making fun of her. She went berserk at the sight of many colorful baby mermaids. Sairas drew a circle around her and the water dispersed. She found herself in a dry bubble, being watched closely by gazillions of mesmerizing mortals.

Spiritual ancestors in human form roamed about gaily, living in co-existence with the water spirits. They had empowered each other and shared their secrets. The city illuminated as far as the eye could see.

The immortal ancestors were walking on two feet but could interchange legs for ns at will. So did the mermaids and mermen.

A tall skinny, decorated mermaid, standing on top of what looked like a dead tortoise, broke into a welcome song.

We welcome you, dear child.
Our home is filled with love.

Whatever you seek, you will get.
Everyone is a friend of yours

We welcome you, dear child
Our home is filled with love and care.

Whatever you seek, you will get.

Everyone is a friend of yours.

Cry no more tears, pain is gone
Some shall stay, some shall return

We welcome you dear child
Our home, is filled with love

Whatever you seek you will get
Everyone is a friend of yours

Cry no more tears, pain is gone
Some shall stay, some shall return

Our home, is filled with love n care
Whatever you seek you will get
Everyone is a friend of yours

Cry no more tears, pain is gone
Some shall stay, some shall return

Chapter 15

Meanwhile, Kojo, who had lured Vera into the sacred land, and watched her disappear with the water spirits, found himself in harm's way. He had been born centuries ago to a human mother and a merman. There was a great rift between the two great guardians of the African continent after centuries of rumors of abusing women. The mermen were banished from venturing outside the waters.

When peace was finally restored, Kojo was rejected by both parties. He worked passionately and wickedly whenever his services were called upon. But he was never fully trusted by anyone since he was half of both worlds.

He became a lost soul and wandered in the wilderness, offering his wicked expertise to whoever desired them. As he crouched eagerly in one of the tallest trees, listening to the menacing moanings of the immortal beings, baying for vengeance.

His eyes crossed, becoming pure white, a urry of ash backs exploded in his head. He saw a beautiful young girl with a group of other girls going to fetch water in a local river. As they filled their buckets, a decorated merman hiding in the water behind some shrubs became attracted to this young girl.

The merman concentrated his eyes on her, and she nearly fell into the water as she responded to his call, but the other girls held her back. In the process, of helping her, she dropped her wrist band into the water. The merman came to the edge of the river and watched her salaciously as she returned to the village.

In the middle of the night, while the girl was sleeping, the merman used the wrist band to wake her up telepathically.

She got up half-naked and followed his mesmerizing voice back to the river. She walked in the darkness as if she was awake.

At the river, she removed her clothes and lay down by the grass. The massive merman crawled out with a strong sexual desire and moaned the whole night as he made love to her.

When it was dawn, she suddenly awoke, not knowing where she was. She gathered her clothing and ran back home. The merman somersaulted a couple of times and disappeared underwater. Each night the merman would lure her to the river and make love to her. One particular night as she returned home, her father was about to come out of the lavatory when he noticed her almost naked. He hid and wandered. He was distraught. She was his only daughter. That following night he did not sleep.

When he heard the door squeaking, he armed himself with a spear. He silently foreshadowed her before realizing she was under some spell.

He observed her performing the same ritual. As she lay on the ground, a giant of a merman stood out of the water and threw himself on top of her.

The father, angry and shaken, ran out of the bush holding his spear high, ready to kill. Just as he was about to thrust the spear through his back, he turned around and shrieked. The father hesitated, but the love of his daughter gave him courage and thrust the spear through his abdomen. The merman screeched in pain and threw the old man into the river. The father sprung up, striking the merman and taking away part of his ear. The young girl suddenly awoke just as the merman was about to kill her father.

She screamed in horror. The merman was distracted. He pulled the spear out of his stomach and was about to kill the old man. Then he paused and stared at her. The look in her eyes mellowed the mermanâ€™s heart. He threw the spear away and dragged the father underwater.
The young girl ran home to call for help, but the father was never seen again. Rumors circulated in the village that she was having an affair with the father and were caught in an uncompromising position. Thatâ€˜s why the merman took him.
The village shunned her, and she endured animosity from the locals. She ran away from home when she discovered she was pregnant. She had caused her mother enough pain already.

For months she traveled with a group of nomads. One night as she slept under a tree, next to a small re, she was awoken by heavy rain and thunderstorms; thatâ€™s when her water broke.
The nomads held her down and tried to assist her. She was bleeding and was in excruciating pain for hours, screaming and shouting.

Finally, the baby popped out into the hands of an elder nomad. But he quickly threw it to the ground when he noticed the baby had no legs but a fin. They all scattered in fear.

The baby wriggled nervously in the rain. The nomads mumbled in prayer, asking for protection and forgiveness. A hyena distracted them, made a creepy sound, laughing as it came out of nowhere, and bit the n, dragging it into the dark. The nomads, out of fear, threw their spears and killed it. The baby, in shock, sprung up, and the fin broke. A young boy with evil tubular eyes and huge lenses stood in front of them, struggling for breath.

The nomads, terrified, ran for cover; they had never witnessed such a scary miracle. The young boy, with such quickness, chased after them in the dark. There were brutal beatings and growling as the nomads cried for help. The unfortunate young girl lay helpless on the ground, too weak to move. She had lost a lot of blood, and she was about to lose consciousness.

The young boy appeared, holding four human heads. He threw them at the mother, his body covered in blood. She struggled to speak, "Kojo, Kojo," and she passed out. He shrieked, his cry echoing far and wide, profound and wrenching.

The water spirits heard the cry, and they knew a powerful curse had been cast. Mama Oyiwas, from deep underneath the ocean, directed lightning to struck him down.

The immortal spirits filled with anger observed him from within their shadows. The lightning missed him by inches as Aragognto Paradza, the immortal warrior, intervened, pushing him aside. Kojo, frightened and spooked, limped off, disappearing into the night, leaving his mother to die.

Chapter 16

Vera finally woke up after weeks of being in the arms of Morpheus. Her hair had grown up to her waist. Two young mermaids joyfully removed dead skin from her body. She twitched, alerting them she was alive. They flickered their eyelashes and continued their work. She slightly opened one eye, afraid of what she might see. The two little mermaids sang softly in a strange language. The touch of their hands felt like warm jelly. It was smooth and relaxing. She was lying in a pond of water surrounded by stunning multiple arrays of glowing in the dark flowers. Some were flashy shades of orange, blue, and red. There was a sea re with a green and yellow glow.

Giant squids and jelly sh of all shapes and sizes glowed smoothly as they swiftly circled the pond.

The tiny underwater island appeared to be artificial. There was an area covered in white sand and blue shells, surrounded by thousands of various types of exotic plants.

In the middle were two small pools of steamy bubbling water. One of the mermaids got out of the pond and turned herself into a mortal being with two legs. She walked across the area and signaled to a non-existent door to open. She then turned into a mermaid and swam away.

Although Vera was in a state, she felt compelled to

talk. "How did she do that?" She startled the other mermaid. The mermaid scornfully gazed at her and swiped her lips with her finger. Vera found herself mute. She was dismayed, and she gestured with her hands in disapproval. The young mermaid quietly pointed her middle finger at her hands, and effortlessly they were bound together by an invisible ligature. She spoke fast and inaudibly.

"Your voice is gone, your hands are bound, no more questions.

I know you want me to tell you our secrets so you can use them against us. No, I am not going to do that. Maybe I should make you blind. You mammals always like to fool us, and all we want is to help you."

She had a small long face with round marble eyes. Her long shiny hair was a mixture of sparkling dark black and yellow stripes. The chromatic scales of her ns felt like hard elastic patches of gum. She jumped out, her n splashing water, and landed on the floor with two legs. She gave Vera a smug look and bolted away.

Chapter 17

While that was happening, Moritz and Boris were regretful and full of guilt. It had been almost a month, and Vera was nowhere to be found.

Each day and night, a search group scouted the vast land. An army helicopter was frequently dispatched from a nearby French base but was to no avail.

"I know she is alive," whispered Freddy. "If she was dead, we should have seen blood or torn clothes, but we have seen nothing till now."

"This is purely bad luck." Moritz moaned. "She lost her family, and now she is gone, maybe dead too."

"Did you say she lost her family? "

"When?" Freddy asked curiously.

"About some six to eight months ago. Why do you ask?" Freddy frowned, his body shrinking in distress. He was in deep thoughts.

"This is not a coincidence, and it sounds more like it was her fate. We might never nd her, but she is alive." He spoke boldly.

"What do you mean? Has she been kidnapped? Is there something you know?" Boris quizzed him.

"How terrible was the tragedy," Freddy asked again.

"Gruesome, the whole family butchered," Moritz said plainly.

"She is alive but in a world of trouble." Freddy barked. "My instincts tell me she has been taken by the spiritual gods, and if not then by the mermaids." He elaborated. Moritz and Boris stared at each other in disbelief. Moritz chuckled, "You believe in that crap, mermaids, and shit."

Freddy withdrew his grin. "This is Africa. We are alive at the mercy of our ancestors. Something must have lured her here. The timeline and the methods used; first, they take blood to cleanse you, then wipe out your whole bloodline, so you have nothing to go back to. We need to visit Nganga, gentlemen.

"What, do you mean? Who is Nganga? Do you want to go to see a witch doctor? Are you superstitious? Come on, Man! Stop joking. She is family to me." Moritz replied angrily.
"You can bring as many helicopters as you want, even a million soldiers. I can tell you this! She will never be found. Unless if we appease the spirits, and if she is lucky.

There is no other way; this is a sacred continent. The longer we wait, the harder it becomes. Grab something that belonged to her and lots of cash. I will get the Jeep." Moritz and Boris stood watching him go.
"Well, I don't think we have anything to lose. We go and do some holla hollers," Moritz jested.
"What if he is right! We are in a foreign country," Boris emphasized.
"Okay then, let's go, and throw some bones. If this shit is real, why wasn't the population ever protected?

If the so-called magic was real, why are the people suffering? Isn't it time someone whips up a few charms, and we are in a better place." Moritz derided.

Chapter 18

Inside a sacred mountain was a hidden unfathomable cave. A small pool of clear blue water lay silently in the middle.

Myriad penumbras of balancing rocks and juxtaposed violet trees, pink Jacarandas percolated along the dolomite rocks. A Miombo rock thrush stood guard. Its piercing whistle was traveling more profound into the depth of the underwater world, alerting the cave keepers. A lantern reflected shadow trailed an old man as he recited an ancient code, seeking access into the underground chamber.

He came to a dead-end with motley rocks that stood as doors on both sides. His voice was low and soft. He placed the lantern in a circle on the ground and began to undress.

The light interjected the colors, and his accentuated monotonous humming created a mysterious movement. He knelt stark naked, spewing bluish and reddish smoke from his mouth.

The miasma engulfed the place, and he found himself worshipping next to the pool of water. He had two pouches filled with liquid around his neck.

He stood next to the water and chanted, Mama Oyiwas, Mama Oyiwas, Mama Oyiwas, The Miombo rock thrush whistled with expectant energy until Mama Oyiwas emerged and transformed into a tall, slim, long haired, young beautiful woman. She had a big headless sh, filled with traditional medicine. As soon as she appeared, he became numb. She circumambulated him, her devilish mixture of greenish and yellowish eyes bickering and radiating.

She frizzled, coerced, and pestered him with her viper tongue. "Blood, blood." She whiffed. She snapped the pouches around his neck and suckled on them. Blood seeped from her mouth, and her facial nerves bloated. "We have taken a new one from across the seas, Vera." Her voice reverberated. He remained bound and stonefaced. She licked his sweaty body and scratched him all over, arousing her appetite. Mama Oyiwas transformed into a mystical creature with two heads.

Out of fear, the old man fell to the ground trembling and whimpering as she sexually abused him. When she was done, she vanished. The old man staggered towards the secret gateway with visible bleeding marks on his back. He reappeared outside the chamber, reinvigorated and feeling youthful.

It was midday, the sky was blue, and the sun was smiling brightly. They drove through a cluster of dilapidated huts.

The dusty, donkey-drawn cart road had never seen a car before; it was bumpy and narrow. Freddy did not say a word, he looked nervous, and that made Moritz and Boris worry.

They took a sharp turn at the end of the road and followed a dry stream that led to a stone canal. The canal ended abruptly and green vegetation sprawled across an arm of the sea.

Mountains stood on either side, silently encompassed by barren land full of sand and stones. A huge tree stood guard into an opening that appeared at the edge of the mountain. Freddy sighed heavily and stopped the car. "We have to walk the rest of the way. Please leave your phones, no gadgets, no cameras. If you have anything to say, say it now. As soon as we make the first step, no talking, it's disrespectful to the spirits." He spoke with a firm voice. Moritz, and Boris sensed his intensity and nodded their heads quietly.

They folded their trousers to their knees and walked barefooted across the rugged surface. In the distance, a drumbeat rhythmically, warning of incoming intruders. When they reached the edge of the compound, a solid foul smell blew into their faces. The sound of the drumbeat became louder and louder. They sneezed and coughed, inhaling the stench. Moritz and Boris suddenly became agitated. Their hairs stood on end, and their knees trembled. They wanted to scream, but their voices had deserted them. Freddy staggered forward with a death stare on his face.

They maneuvered along a tiny two-lane strip paved with python skins and skeletons of scary creatures. There was glittering oil sprinkled on portions of the skins. Jars filled with liquids, organs, and dead animals lined the pathway.

A gigantic crocodile skull hung above the entrance, which was decorated by chilling animal skulls. There were hundreds of dead monkey feet, pangolin scales, and tails of hyena.

They crossed a white and red piece of cloth, laid midway. And as if possessed and in a trance, they began to jiggle to the beat. From inside, six pairs of ghostlike images watched
and marked them like hunted animals.

They shook and wriggled for hours until they were in their undergarments. A mysterious dark Blanket of smoke enveloped the area. The clouds, stars, and the moon seized to exist. A sharp faster drum beat took over, and three skinny half-naked men painted with white paint emerged. They blindfolded them and put a noose around their necks, dragging them inside.

Trickles of water fell on their heads. They led them through dungeons and halls of caves. Sharp stones bruised their feet.

They walked up and down, deeper into the mountain and across streams of water. They stood for a while in a room blistering with heat. Someone pushed their knees down and removed the blindfolds.

They found themselves kneeling in front of Nganga. The place was surprisingly clean, brightly lit, and a semi-circle shrine neatly arranged. They were skulls of creatures staring at them.

Nganga was a young man dressed in a clean red shirt. The three men were not convinced but were afraid to talk for fear of losing their voices. Nganga quickly got up and smiled at something behind them. He threw some white powder over them, and they turned in anticipation of something. A shadow flew above them, creating a trail of dust. An older Nganga wearing strips of wild animal skins appeared. He had feathers of birds on his head. He wore various ornaments of crocodile, lion, leopard, and squirrel teeth around his neck. Beads and rattling seedpods covered his arms and legs. His face and body had red and white markings. In the middle of his white afro hair, a chicken foot was perfectly tucked in. Without paying any attention to his guests, he squat-ted opposite them and started playing dice with some bones. He mumbled and chattered to himself as he threw tiny bones on a mat. He fell back screaming, fear on his face.

Moritz, Boris, and Freddy followed his movements with their eyes wide.

"Muyedzo don't just stand there; give the visitors food and beer to drink and eat." He spoke English fluently. The men contradicted themselves and shook their heads. Nganga was not pleased with their gestures. He sprung up to his feet and lectured them.

"How dare you deny my ancestors?" He screamed and spat on the floor. His voice became intense and inaudible.

"Ninyi vyura wadogo watatu, mnaingia nyumbani kwa Sangoma na kukataa kula chakula chake. Huna heshima, ninapaswa kukugeuza kuwa kobe."

(You three little frogs, you come into Nganga's house and refuse to eat his food. You have no respect; I should turn you into tortoises)

He took out some polished bones inside a headless fish and threw them on the ground. A bonfire erupted in the middle of the room, touching the top of the ceiling, and immediately simmered.

Muyedzo hurriedly saved them while disparaging them. "I want to warn you. Don't you dare to disrespect Sekuru, eat your food immediately before he gets angry?" He placed down two big tortoise shells crammed with meat and sima and a hairy horn filled with a milky drink. The three men ate and drank like hungry lions. Consumed in the tasty food, the Nganga yelled.

"Je! Ni kuzimu gani, hiyo ilitokeaje, sijawahi kuona kitu kama hiki hapo awali."

(What the hell, how did that happen? I have never seen anything like this before.) They stopped grazing and gawked at him. He lifted his head, with an intimidating look on his face.

Somehow he was not convinced, he sprinkled some liquid and cupped the bones and blew into them. He slowly threw them again as if expecting a different result. With his heart thudding fast, he muttered, and communicated with the still bones. The bones shimmered, reflecting a dull light, and blood appeared on one of them. Nganga stumbled and clasped his hands, visibly shocked. Drumbeats suddenly filled the room. Three young women covered in colorful material jumped in the middle, and the place became a pulsating, frenzied dance area. The women were erratically hopping, shaking, and ululating, in a circle. They danced for hours nonstop. Meanwhile, Nganga lay back, his eyes wide open, his body jerking. He looked as if he had entered a spiritual realm.

The men tucked themselves in a corner and observed science in the making. A gust of wind swirled, levitating Nganga. The dance floor cleared, and the drumbeats reduced to a light tapping sound. A spiritual voice of authority echoed.

Nganga was unconscious, levitated the air. *"Kusahau kuhusu Vera, bado yuko hai, lakini sio muda mrefu. Wengi wanatamani damu yake. Dhambi za mababu zake. Yeye hataonekana tena, milele."* (Forget about Vera she is still alive, but not for long. Many crave her blood. Sins of her ancestors. She will never be seen again)

After the words were spoken, Nganga fell to the ground. A cold, burning fog filled the room.

Freddy, Moritz, and Boris staggered out of the cave, almost naked. They found their clothes thrown on the ground with a pyramid of stones next to them. They looked as if they had just walked out of an allnight paty. No one said a word. What they had just witnessed and heard was unfathomable. Their beliefs, perceptions, and cultural values were hijacked and scorched.

Boris trembled with fear. Moritz was awe-stricken; he experienced a change of energy. He had been cleansed and somehow longed for more. Freddy strode in front, pretending to have handled it well. They walked in silence, and when they had reached a certain point, a fresh breeze woke them.

That is when they realized they were naked. They hastily put on their clothes and walked as fast as they could towards where they had parked the car. Strangely, they seemed to have bypassed the place. A long narrow path covered with dried cow dung appeared from nowhere. There was no sign of the car.

Boris began to sob. He was too overwhelmed. No one cared to soothe him. The previous events had touched a nerve. They walked along the path without saying a word until a young boy in cattle drawn cart gave them a ride. "I should never have gone there; I will never be the same again. I see ghosts, ghosts, everywhere." Boris mumbled.

When they got to the camp, the Jeep was parked next to Moritz's hut. They gasped, but nothing seemed strange anymore. Freddy warned them not to talk about it for the next three days or else they would go mad.

Chapter 19

Vera realized she could talk and was able to walk unassisted. A floating orchid decorated with various fruits swung towards her, packed with heavenly fruits. She remained spooked, rooted in the pool. Her legs wobbled, hunger and fear weakkneed her. A mixture of clay and some type of algae had been plastered on her body. Her hands were numb, and her nostrils clogged. Sarais, together with four older mermaids, became visible. He walked without fear as he approached her in a polite manner.

"It's good to see that you are feeling much better. We were getting worried. It's been almost a month since you lay dormant. You don't respond well to our hospitality, do you?"

The four older mermaids stood levitated in a semi-circle. They had round eyes inside bigger eyes that swiveled, radiating and releasing puffs of multi-colored powder. Their heads were covered in oversized white hoods, not a single part of their body was visible. They swayed silently from side to side, waiting for directives.

"You will be under their tutelage," he continued. „They are known as Mama Oyiwas. Follow their instructions carefully; they are not very forgiving."

One of them moved forward; a long thin hand protruded and held her by the shoulder. Vera felt a zap going through her body. Childhood memories came flashing back. Everything she ever did or saw in her life vividly played in her head. Mama Oyiwas breathed into her, and her mind went blank. She became like a toddler. When she opened her eyes, it was as if she had just been born. She glanced around childishly with her innocent eyes and playfully attempted to touch her robe. A much bigger eye with patches of hair protuding shot out. The fierce look made her chuckle, and she backed off. A large sea horse emerged and started spreading worms and eggs on an enormous sea leaf. It then let out sh, shrimps, lobsters, crabs, and oysters. The mermaid coaxed her to start consuming. She ate everything on the menu and immediately fell asleep in the pond. Mama Oyiwas created a bubble around her and left her to rest.

When she woke up, she had developed the mind of a juvenile. She could see further than the normal eye, and her head kept twitching. She was baffled by a continuous rattling sound in her ears.

Mama Oyiwas showed up alone, and as soon as she stood in front of her, she quadrumvirate. Four Mama Oyiwas circumvented her. Vera squeaked and plunged into the water.

She resurfaced with seaweed in her mouth; her body wear had turned into a light blue costume, with glittering silver linings. Mama Oyiwas levitated and glided her into a maze of darker, deeper tunnels. A thousand blistering eyes roamed and guarded the caves, emitting multihued misty fumes. The energy and atmosphere were mysteriously spiritual. There was an eerie silence except for a low, indistinct continuous sizzling sound. Vera chuckled, and she was instantly made mute. An illuminating, gigantic octopus called Zuju held her up with its tentacles attached to every part of her body. She was in a spiritual, mythical operating theatre. She felt sharp waves of pain penetrating through her feet. There was a quick burst of the blood being siphoned and a similar surge being pumped in. Vera writhed, and briefly, all her organs were visible to the naked eye. The veins contracted and expanded, illuminating a bluish light. Her body sucked in, squeezed into a bundle, and outstretched, doubling her normal size. Each drop of blood that was drained revealed a dark history of a cursed generation, repudiating sins of their forefathers, therefore, reneging on a solemn promise regarding the future of their offspring that was forged between their ancestors and an ancient witch. Vera was taken back to the 1600th century when her great Portuguese grandfather was born. The events were taking place right in front of her. It was a real flashback. She saw how her ancestors had lived their lives and how their family grew from two to twenty great grandfathers. Abnormally most of them had died under mysterious circumstances, and some had suffered cruelly to unknown diseases. She saw the atrocities her family had committed during that period. She viewed how her great grandfather joined an illfated voyage and how he was rescued by Queen Mama Wata.

The process was repeated ten times until all the organs reacted appropriately. Her heart had an added layer of reinforced ber coated around it.

The new blood created a tough band of the extra thick tissue on the outside, making her body impermeable and flexible. In the darkness, a wide drooling tongue slobbered over her legs and waist, leaving a yellowish slime. It hardened, compressing her feet and merging them as one. The yellowish slime enveloped her from the waist down, and a transparent padded sheet glowed as the the femurs, fibulas, patellas, and the tibias dissolved and formed one large solid rubbery bone. The mermaid fin. Her whole body lit up, and fireworks exploded inside her. The darkness twinkled and luminesced in celebration. Vera was out cold, her face as pale as death. A ball of smoke filled the area as a spotlight tracked a huge spiritual figure dressed in a black robe with an invisible face. A bright light lit up, exposing Vera to the unseen eyes. Singing and traditional drums erupted. Voices of women ululating, stomping the ground with their feet, and clapping their hands echoed. The invisible face stood silently scrutinizing her. As the beats be- came louder, the black robe giant rhythmically shook violently, as if possessed. The black robe jumped up and down, swirling and rolling on the floor. The beats became intense, and the whole place shook. A spiritual voice reverberated, drowning the drumbeats. Other unidentified guests humbly hummed and thudded with their feet. It was unpredictable energy that seemed foreign even to the undersea world. At that moment, the octopus and its tentacles mysteriously dissolved, leaving Vera high on spiritual ecstasy. She levitated, ritually dancing, wriggling back and forth, thrusting her head and hands forward. Her body was rhythmically loosening up to the sound of a lead drum. She circled, rolled, and tangled, opening her spiritual spirit to what was beyond her spiritual body. The fin became female legs again. The performance went on for weeks until the immortal spiritual powers were satisfied. Her blood was kept in the puku of an invisible golden dolphin.

Chapter 20

Not all spirits were in agreement with the procedure. There was a group known as the water runners, the Naiteru-kop. They were tall, slim, and unpredictable. As mortal beings, they were known for their fighting skills using short spears.

Their athletic abilities and strength had left a lot of wild animals panting. They had carried that tradition into the water world after being accepted by the water spirits.

Then there was the Mbokomu, which was a tribe of women. Most fathers would take their daughters to be groomed to become wives of Kings, great warriors, and chiefs. Since most men had been wiped out or enslaved, they turned their anger into feared fighters. They trusted no one, and their belief was to maim first and then ask questions. Because of their beauty and mannerism, it was easier for them to penetrate the enemy and strike from within.

The Mbokomu and the Naiteru-kop repelled the idea of purifying the blood of a lineage serial killer and turn her into a weapon of mass destruction against her own kind. They preferred to have her suffer a painful death." What If she comes back to destroy us."

They had argued. But the water spirits had the last say; after all, it was their Kingdom.

The disgruntled parties walked away loathing and

offended. The Mbokomu and the Naiteru-kop felt like intruders and longed to have a land of their own. They arranged a
secret palaver inside the insulated belly of a huge female whale called Tunia.

Ahosi, Amanirenas, Nzinga, and Kaigirwa, the most fearless Mbokomu warriors, met with Tinbukti, Kampande, Njoya, and Askum from the Naiteru-kop tribe. Ahosi used her beauty to hypnotize the whale, which was well hidden in an enclave between two dome-shaped icebergs. They stood opposite each other, battle-ready. The belly was big enough to t in a
hundred strong men. Sea butterflies glittered, leaving a trail of blinking lights.

"We have overstayed our welcome," Ahosi spoke firmly. "We are not known as cowards; we should be among our people, our descendants," Tinbukti added.

"We mean no harm to the water spirits; they have been great hosts. We have shared our secrets with them, but I think the time has come to stand on our own." Askum said elatedly.

"What we witnessed today was of utmost disrespect.
A bloodline that murdered millions of our people, our
husbands, and sent us cowering like cowards. Now they propose to grant her eternal life and in line to be bestowed with
powers that none of us possess. I say rebellion." Amanirenas spoke with a lot of anger.

"They want to use her to fight our battles; that is an insult to us. We have gained enough strength and knowledge; we should go out and do to them what they did to us." Kaigirwa declared.

"We need a contact from the mainland, someone who understands us," Tinbukti suggested.

"I might have one," said Nzinga. She was the youngest,
the
shortest, and the prettiest. She looked innocent and na-
ive,
but that hand had already taken a thousand lives.
"Well then, let's meet again when the contact has been
established. In the meantime, we stay low," rumbled
Kampande.

Chapter 21

After months of recuperation and undergoing cultural indoctrination, Vera felt like a half-edged mermaid. She thought she no longer had restrictions. Unbeknownst to her, an army of invisible giants called the Bhakidas kept her under surveillance. She paced the sea in full of admiration of the place. She came across a food bank where they had whale nests. The whales would come and give their milk to the dwellers of the Kingdom and regurgitated tonnes of fish. Baby mermaids wandered around with sharks and dolphins as pets. There was an enclosure for land animals that had been turned into sea creatures. These included Giraffes, Zebras, Lions, elephants, rhinos, and many more roam freely.

The Kingdom was created on multiple subterranean sea floors. Mermaid and mermen had the power to make themselves invisible.

They could control water with mind and hand. The powers were granted according to their duties and length of existence. Those assigned to controlling the borders of the Kingdom possessed seven powers.

They could create and control ice.

They could freeze water or cool it down.

They were bestowed with powers to start a fire and summon lightning. Their favorite ability was to control the wind as they could capsize or divert unwanted vessels. On land, they could boil or evaporate water. Vera had the power to live underwater and swim faster than any fish. She came across a group of spiritual leviathans sitting around a fire, reminiscing and guffawing. When they felt her presence, they turned and stared at her suspiciously.

There was a system of classification where immortal spiritual beings that used to be Kings and Queens had designated areas.

Chosen Immortal warriors stood guard outside palaces as an honor to their tribes.

She had transformed pretty well. Her face had shrunk proportionally, and her eyes pierced, radiating a greenish color. Long hair weaved up to her ankles. A mixture of strawberries and cream was the tone of her voice as she swiveled her lips.

Her slender body with a selected inch-perfect muscle stood toned, filled with innocence. Her demeanor was calm, cautious, and content.

"Scattered seeds weaken the bond," Sairas said as he appeared beside her. Her small eyes popped out, attracting Sairas's attention, and she said softly.

"It's a breath of fresh air, seeing all these majestic creations."

Sairas sighed, „It will be a great pleasure to take you on a tour of our majestic continent. He repeated. „What would appease your eyes?"

"You lead, I follow." Her voice blossomed the sleeping owers.

"Come with me. In a breath of fresh air, I will show you the countryside."

"Countryside, what is that supposed to be."

"Natural beauty, you will soon find out."

They torpedoed deeper and wider into the waters passing through boulders of sculptured rocks suspended in the water. They could cover a distance of a thousand kilometers in a matter of minutes.

They reached a certain region, and the color of the water became yellowish and smelt of dead owers. Vera sneezed to the amusement of Sairas. A wall of a long dark rock blocked their way. Sairas blinked, and the wall cracked open.

"Leave no doubt in your head; feel it, and it will be done."

Vera awed in silence as her eyes grew bigger and bigger. She looked like a child who had just tasted candy for the first time. A sharp, bright light twinkled through the water, causing a rift between a cool breeze and the sun that dazzled her. A sea of substantial Victorian villas Spread out over a wide area. They were spaciously built with manicured green grass and backyard gardens of inflorescences. Vera wondered where the light was coming from.

"It's only an illusion that makes you feel you are closer to the surface." Sairas clarified.

"Look, can you see the clouds?" Vera winced; the metamorphosis and the sun's rays had partially blinded her. Sairas smiled, his eyes musing on her distinguishable face. She gazed in admiration. He stopped and held his hands up, showing his invisible security checks. When they got cleared, the water divided, creating a space between their knees to above their heads. The blue sky and the sun illuminated as if they were walking on land. Vera was ecstatic to see the endless body of water bouncing on a surface separated by thin
air, and higher above white clouds raced towards the

horizon. „The air is dry and salty," she said with her nostrils pulsating.

"Does it feel like home? We are in what you call the pyramids of the Atlantic Sea. From here, we can go down to the Indian Ocean and up to the Red Sea. Our borders stretch to the Mediterranean Sea." Sairas savored. Vera had no idea what he was talking about. „You lead I follow."

Sairas drooled. „In the aftermath of the invasion of this once impenetrable African continent, sold out by greedy, soulless, and selfish descendants. No one has ever known peace, and no one will until a continental cultural ritual has been carried out and all binding contracts revoked. The mystic rulers of the undersea world and the immortal spiritual powers of the land will never adhere to such contracts. They are willing to destroy their own and rebuilt a new nation with untainted blood. The continent has been crippled and destabilized by war, hunger, corruption, false gods, and diseases. A dark cloud from across the Atlantic has its sight on this virgin land. Soon the world will be fighting a battle for humanity, men, and riches. What used to be natural will seize and become a burden. A mind can easily be manipulated and tamed as long as you crave what is beyond

your reach. Evil powers have been bestowed upon cloggedminded, plainly sinister dark forces. The world bleeds of contrition; its core has been er

oded by termites."

His tone was torn apart. Vera glided calmly, listening to every single word.

"Our spiritually guided beacon is in disarray. The spiritual souls of our people have become too scattered.

The bond has become weakened, and scattered seeds weaken the bond. The strength of the African continent is a spiritual magnetic ball that feeds on each and every individual.

When one disconnects, its power decreases. Masses have migrated, enslaved, and many more will fall ill, thrust upon us by those who seek what we possess. A happy soul stays home; a sad soul goes astray.

If you seek to destroy, sow chaos, create a remedy, a desperate soul will fall for anything. „We might have lost the battle but not our continent. The time has come to awaken the sleeping giants." He spoke with authority as his face changed shades.

"Are we expecting trouble?" She asked innocently.

He smiled, vanished, and reappeared a distance away from her. She mumbled and bubbled, struggling to keep up with him.

Aragognot Paradza summoned a hundred thousand men to scour the land. He breezed along the perimeters of the guarded spiritual wall, knowing fully well, he had no chance of penetrating it. Vera had been taken by the water spirits, with the help of Nzambi a Mpungu immortal spirits.

The Nzambi a Mpungu, were known as the gods of the earth. When they joined forces with the gods of the water, other spiritual mediums disowned them. The Nzambi a Mpungu and the water spirits could change their location with a snap of anger. Their combined power made it harder to discover. They had a few points of entry that could only be granted by an immortal spirit-based inside.

Aragognot Paradza planted immortal spirits, spies, in the camp among human beings.

They moved around as villagers, child soldiers, wounded victims, and helpers.

Chapter 23

Freddy and Moritz had not talked for days, afraid of discussing the inevitable problem.

They stood next to the Jeep, drinking hot tea in large metal mugs. Reluctantly Moritz spoke, „have you woken up from the dream yet? I still cannot believe what I saw and heard. It just doesn't make sense." Freddy breathed silently without saying a word. „If these so-called spirits can come into our world and kidnap our people, we should be able to go into their world and rescue them." Freddy burst out laughing. "You believe what are you saying?" He continued laughing.

"She is gone, man, only they get to decide what to do."
"I'm sure Nganga can help us." Freddy's face changed.
"Never mention that name again, you hear; it's taboo."
There were sudden loud noise and a strong rush of wind; trees swerved and rustled. Freddy and Moritz cowered.
"What was that?"
"Probably to do with something you just said," Freddy answered irritably. Immortal spirits frantically left their positions in nearby trees to report what they had heard.
"What's wrong captain, are you afraid of a generator," a middle aged soldier chewing sugar cane said as he approached them.

"This place is becoming unbearable. Machines are breaking down, people falling sick mysteriously. There is a bad spirit around here."
He took a mean look at Moritz and smirked.
"Soon, this place will be overrun by strange foreign diseases. I thought I would let you know."
As he walked away, Moritz and Freddy sighed with fear in their eyes. Boris came out holding his luggage. He looked disheveled and disoriented.
"I'm going back home. I want to get out of this filthy voodoo place." He had grown a beard and had dark circles around his eyes.
"Freddy, please drive me to the airport. I will die if I stay here a minute longer. I need to go home to my mother."
"Calm down, Boris, we are leaving together."
"My mission is complete. I will never return. You, Vera, that Nganga cursed me. I know you wanted me dead. You wanted to sacrifice me."
"What are you talking about?" Moritz interrupted him.
"Shadows beat me up in the night; scary creatures suck my blood. I can't take it anymore. Please get me out of here," he begged them.
A twister of air picked up dust and leaves, It swirled around them, and soon there were a dozen twisters around them. Chief Chirau materialized in front of them. The three men backed off in fear.
"Hello, gentlemen, can you please escort me to Vera's room."
His voice was as clear as crystal and as cold as ice. He looked at them like a cyborg."
"We believed she is the reincarnation of an evil empire."
The men pointed towards Vera's door. He whizzed into

her room, and it began to rain heavily. The men stood in the rain, observing the door. Inside, Chief Chirau went through her belongings, taking her hairbrush, photos of her late family, a bottle of her favorite whisky, and one of her blouses.

There was a sudden strike of lighting, sending Freddy, Moritz, and Boris ducking under the Jeep. The rain stopped, and the sun came out shining. It was as if nothing had just happened. The earth was dry, and people were going about their business. Boris broke down; he was crying. He was crying and shouting.

„What did I tell you? Did you see what just happened? If we stay here, they will butcher us, man."

„I think you are right, Boris; we should get going. Freddy, get us out of here. We will pay you whatever is necessary," Moritz spoke nervously. Freddy hissed, „I have never seen anything like this before. The gods must be angry. Can you take me with you?" Moritz was caught by surprise by the question.

„If you have the necessary paperwork, we can arrange something," he stammered. „You have been of great help to us," Moritz stated.

„Good, that is what I wanted to hear. Get your bags so let's meet in ve minutes." Freddy ran to his tent to collect his already packed bag. When he returned, Moritz and Boris were open-mouthed, the car tires were slashed. They could sense and hear a pack of unseen mystifying hyenas laughing and growling around them. They huddled together, kicking and swinging their bags as if they were under attack.

„Captain, what's going on over there." A female soldier asked in confusion.

"Move away, you will you get beaten."

"Beaten by what? Are you people ok?" She stood laughing at them.
"Watch out, run, run," Freddy shouted, and the growling stopped. The men appeared stupe ed. She gazed at them in astonishment.
"Cut down on your smoking captain," she giggled and walked away.

Chapter 24

Aragognot Paradza created a bubble, and Chief Chirau fantasized about being escorted into the spiritual realm. He carried Vera's belongings in a small pouch made out of pangolin scales. Chief Chirau was gratified to have been the chosen one. None of his other chiefs had been in the spiritual realm before.

He witnessed the anguish on the immortal soldiers' faces. They were bitter for having allowed the invaders to trick them. They knew they had betrayed generations to come. When they sensed his mortal being, they embraced him and instilled their spirit in him. They made him stronger and fearless.

Chief Chirau saw warriors and famous names he had heard of.

He oscillated, overcome with joy, and tears swelled in his eyes.

As Chief Chirau wandered in the courtyard with his new imaginary buddies, even the immortal beings had become suspicious of their descendants.

Vera's possessions, her comb, blouse, photos, and a whisky bottle floated in front of Chief Kandagu and Mbuya Hanevi. Gold dust rained on her stuff, and distorted image ashes of Vera transmitted. In annoyance, Mbuya Hanevi threw another cloud of mixed gold and silver dust, a blitz of sparkles emitted, causing the faceless to thud and hum.

The hieroglyphics transformed their emotions into grave and repulsive expressions. The sparkles were an ancient myth to the spiritual beings, considered as a sign of a forged alliance between the dark spirits and the water spirits, seeking a legion of supernatural powers in order to penetrate orbital fields of invisible, sacred planets for ultimate control of the universe.

„Nzambi a Mpungu, Nzambi a Mpungu, Nzambi a Mpungu," the name of the feared spiritual God echoed. Mbuya Hanevi lifted her golden encrusted knobkerrie; other spiritual beings did the same too, a unanimous decision had been reached. Fiery drumbeats erupted, thudding and humming rebounded, deafening
the spiritual vault.

Aragognot Paradza was ordered to coerce Nganga for insight into the world of water spirits. Nganga had clandestinely, known to them, ingurgitated since inception, herbs, knowledge, and powers from known dark worlds. He covertly liaised with them in return for magical powers and healing remedies.

Aragognot Paradza amalgamated thousands of spiritual war ready warriors and marshaled them in the vicinity of Nganga's compound. It was a spiritual whirlwind race among the immortal beings eager to restore lost pride. A flurry blizzard of dust cyclones, gales, windstorms, chased by willy willies left behind uprooted trees and fine particles of sand. The sun felt the turmoil, not to be outdone, sneaked out and foreshadowed the perpetrators scorching everything in its way.

The sudden commotion trembled the earth and activated nature alarms. A cloud burst poured down, deluging and clogging dry valleys.

Chapter 25

Although Kojo seemed vulnerable and polite, there was something hidden behind his visage of politeness. He squatted on top of a rock in the middle of a plain eld, consumed in despair. He felt shunned because of his mixed nature.

He had no allegiance to anyone, and both worlds despised him.

He was a lost soul, wandering aimlessly in search of a host. A furious army of immortal beings ashed past him, leaving him ducking and frustrated.

Aragognto Paradza noticed him and smirked. Chief Chirau, under a spell of the spirits, whizzed past Kojo chasing after the immortal. Kojo grinned; he jumped and discreetly trod on his heels. He was interested in being part of the raucous, fueled by his morbid fascination with vicious spiritual punishments.

Chapter 26

The door of the hut was ripped off by strong winds as Freddy and Moritz watched in fear of the heavy rains pouring outside. Boris cupped his ears and hunched in one corner, murmuring, wishing he was back home. The rain was aggressive, the winds were fearsome, and it seemed to be coordinated.

Each time gusts of wind circled, a hush whoosh was generated, followed by a lighting strike and heavy raindrops. The ritual was repeated a couple of times. Moritz approached the entrance stealthily. He glanced sideways, paying attention to the falling rain. As soon as he got it, he smiled.

"Listen carefully; something is going on here," he yelled. Freddy stared at him with worriment shown in his eyes. "The modus operandi is quite an obvious right," he smiled mischievously at him. „It's some form of communication; something is about to happen."

"Water, wind, and lighting are communicating. Are you going bonkers like your friend?" Freddy berated him. „Just take time to listen, 1,2,3,4,5, a gust of wind whoosh, thunder, heavy raindrops." Freddy's eyes opened wide and his ears twisted.

"Uh! You are right," he stammered. "This is Hondo yeMudzimu!"

"What is that supposed to mean?" Freddy was silent as he listened again, „Spiritual warfare."

"Spiritual warfare, between which spirits?"

He shook his head, „I have no idea; it's going to be nasty."

Suddenly Boris whimpered and growled. He was shaken violently and thrown against the wall, falling with a thud. Freddy and Moritz watched in confusion; they took cautious steps to check on him. Unexpectedly he rose, pinned against the wall. His face had transformed into a fiery nonhuman. The creature had a big ear on top of its head. Its eyes were on the side and had two holes in the middle of it's face. Freddy and Moritz fell to the ground in fear.

"Why do you seek Vera? Why do you seek Vera?" The voice came through the two holes and sounded like a broken underwater megaphone.

"Never return; death awaits you." A flash of light blinded them, and they squirmed in pain.

Chapter 27

Sairas became agitated, his eyes glowed, and his head jerked multiple times. Small green dots developed on his left palm. He rubbed the dots, and tiny crystals fell out.

"The immortal spirits are ravaging the earth, feeling ashamed of the loss of their land," he smirked. Each time the east immortal beings converge with the north and the western tribes, their cries of humiliation can shake the continent. You are the savior of the human race."

" Human race, why would I do that? I would like to see a human." At that moment, cyclones raced past them. „Somebody is bored, who is doing that. Come, let's turn back. You have seen enough."

"It was about to get interesting," Vera sulked.

"How is our émigré holding up?"

"We are on target, chief commander."

"Excellent, after the second transformation, she will be a lethal weapon. Invisible at will, spit re like a dragon, move weapons with a twitch and annihilate our conquerers for good.

Keep an eye on her. Her mind must forever be nullified."

"I have her under control, chief commander." Before Sarais finished talking, Chief commander Monko had already retreated into his chambers.

He was a heavily built merman; his upper body, just

like his praetorians, was darker than his lower body. Because of his imposing figure, shrewdness, and fearless character, water spirits from other continents never dared to challenge them.
That might have been the reason why foreign mortal beings had been manipulated and send over to invade the African continent.

Chapter 28

Aragognot Paradza and his spiritual infantry of disgruntled, and hapless immortal beings, billeted in the rain within the boundaries of Nganga's forti ed compound. They could not penetrate the protected border created by the water spirits and the renegade immortal spirits. Nganga hardly ventured outside the perimeters of the enclave of the mountain, without consent from his spiritual masters. Only a mortal human being could access his place of work seeking a cure or to cast a spell on their rivals. Aragognot Paradza needed Chief Chirau for that task. But Chief Chirau was a day away

running on foot with Kojo stalking him.

"I know where Vera is," said Kojo as he appeared run- ning next to Chief Chirau. "But I will only tell you if Aragognot Paradza accepts me into the team." Chief Chirau screeched and stopped.

Aragognot Paradza came out of Chief Chirau and revealed himself. "I saved you once, twice is a burden."

"I was just being helpful. I had no idea why they wanted her so badly, but I brought her here."

"That's impossible, we cannot go over our boundaries."

"But I can, you forget I am half you half me."

"You will never be one of us, you are an outcast." Aragognot Paradza's massive body looked as if he was talking to a toddler.

Chief Chirau in his human form watched perplexed as he witnessed two spirits in discussion.

"How did you cross over?"

"Will you accept me as I am?"

"That's not for me to decide, either you tell me or this is your end."

"If you kill me, you will never know the secret, we could keep this between us."

"He grabbed him by the throat and lifted him.

"You don't negotiate with a spiritual warrior. Your time has come." Before he could snap his neck, Chief Chirau intervened. He stammered, "We need him, if we want Vera back.

He has connections to the underwater world."

"Actually I do," said Kojo. Aragognot Paradza grunted. "She is beautiful, I could arrange a meeting," Kojo was a conniving little fellow.

"I don't trust you. How did you cross the seas? Well I met a guy, he is a commander of the water spirits and he begged for my services."

"A commander begged for your services?" Aragognot Paradza laughed. "He must be a weak one." Kojo heaved sighed heavily, as he remembered how Sairas had coerced him and threatened him with his worst nightmare. The bite of a hyena.

Aragognot Paradza withdrew his dagger, "How about your beautiful friend from the underwater world?" Chief Chirau intervened again. "Why don't you want me to kill him?"

"I think he is very useful my chief. We should meet his friend and judge for ourselves." Chief Chirau insisted calmly. Aragognot Paradza reluctantly agreed. "Any funny tricks, you will nd your head in my pouch." Kojo unwilling and jittery took them to his secret meeting place.

Chapter 29

Vera loved being pampered, and treated to delicious tuna and caviar. Occasionally her actions were erratic and she had major mood swings. Sometimes, she behaved as if she was a kid and would sulk and refuse to eat. She still struggled to understand why she did not have a mermaid tail or special powers. They were preparing her for the nal transformation.

She stood in a glass box lled with a thick and slippery greenish substance. A group of mermaids tended to her hair, rolling it and covering it with sea plants and corals, turning it into an arti cial island. An electrical current zapped continuously in the room producing a blurred blue light.

Mermaids love fooling around and being naughty. They pricked her with cactus spines and rubbed bull frog saliva on her belly. They dyed her hair into multiple colors until they settled for pink. Her hands were bound and her mouth sealed with a jelly sh. They tittered at their own jest, as Vera derided their actions.

Sairas, Mama Oyiwas and a host of other members appeared suddenly around the glass box. As Mama Oyiwas got closer to Vera, she stuck her nose out, catching the scent of a weird smell. Mama Oyiwas backed off and quickly closed the lid of the glass box, giving her a stern look.

Chief commander Monko and his army of protectors

glided in, and the place became silent. He nodded at Sairas and he in turn nodded at Mama Oyiwas. The glass box was filled with a colorless, odorless, and high- ly ammable gas. The aim was to create a second layer of skin that was capable of resisting ames and other hot objects. Some form of bacteria was added, that ate away soft particles of the gas, leaving the hardened and strong particles perfectly intact. An acidic substance was infused, changing the color of the new armor and killing off the bacteria.

Mama Oyiwas snapped her ngers, a monstrous color- ful medusae jelly sh unveiled itself.

It attached its tentacles armed with stinging cells to her body giving off sparks, and mushroomed her in its translucent rudimental stomach. It used its tentacles for propulsion, whirled and disappeared. She was going to stay for thirty days insulated in the stomach of the jellyfish.

Chapter 30

Kojo led the way as the immortal Aragognot Paradza invisibly escorted him. Chief Chirau sang and praised the ancestors as he danced closely following them. They came to an ever green area with plenty of trees and wild owers. Kojo trail blazed through sharp thorns, and thickets until he reached a vast eld of tall grass. Hidden in the middle was a thick short tree with wide spaced out branches. He propped himself up and suspiciously checked to see if no one was following them. In the middle of the tree stump was a big hole carefully covered by a uniform tree bark.

"This is the meeting place, let's see how fast you are." He lifted the cover and slid down the hole in jubilation. Aragognot Paradza went in next followed by Chirau Chirau. They dropped down among a bush of exotic owers. It was a garden in paradise. There was no clear passage for the sun to illuminate, but the place was full of sunshine.

"You need to stay out of sight otherwise she will not come out."

"We are to meet a woman."

"Yes from the Mbokomu warriors tribe." Aragognot Paradza's eyes grew wider, he instantly became invisible. Kojo was thrilled

"He is scared of women," he gigg- led jocosely.

Chief Chirau poked him with his knobkerrie, "A long time ago, men fought and died for their women and many women died and fought for their men. Everyone of us has lost someone we once loved. You have never experienced love have you?" Kojo became gloomy.

"What is your signal for her to come out?" He bit his lips, walked over and stood on a at stone in the corner of the garden. He stayed like that for a while and then did a handstand. The prints of his feet and the prints of his hands and his weight had to match what was already preprogrammed.
A portion of the ground in the middle parted, exposing two small pot holes. In one of the potholes they were three baby bonito sh. He held them one by one looking into their eyes and released them into the second hole.

He walked back over to Chief Chirau, "Now we wait."
"For how long?"
"When she is ready she will come, might take a day, might take a week or even a month. I have all the time in the world."
"So do I," Chief Chirau responded. For four days Aragognot Paradza stood staring at the pothole without blinking. Kojo spent most of the time, tending to his feet removing dead thorns from underneath them.
Chief Chirau mixed some ower seeds, with he had ext- racted from one of the trees. He added green leaves and drank the toxic brew showing honor and reverence to his ancestral spirits. Immortal spirits were known to be brutal if they felt disrespected.
Chief Chirau was aware of it and he knew continuously honoring them would calm Aragognot Paradza's

temper, although in this case his spiritual thoughts were millions of miles away.

Chapter 31

Since the Mbokomu and the Naiteru-kop tri- be had joined forces with the water spirits, they had lost access to the powerful ancestral spirits. Inside Tunia the whale, Ahosi, Amanirenas, Nzinga and Kai- girwa covertly met with Tinbukti, Kampande, Njoya and Askum.

"I did not expect that to happen. They inserted her in- side an invisible jelly sh. Those things are the most dif- cult to trace. She could be in anywhere." Nzinga spoke bitterly.

"How are we going to nd her?" Kampande asked.

"From what I know, after a week, it has to reveal itself to recharge its strength."

"I am sure Sarais has a way of keeping in contact with it."

"But how do we nd out? Ahosi responded.

There was a moment of silence. "What if its still in the same place? I don't think Mama Oyiwas would let it out of her sight and don't forget the Bhakidas are always near," said Nzinga

"Thats a good point, I think we need to keep our eyes on the Bhakidas, after all they are responsible for all the top secrets." Tinbukti divulged.

"Any luck with the outside world? Askum asked gently. an answer." Amanirenas assured them. "We need to be vigilant and cautious, we don't want to raise any alarms. We are at the mercy of our hosts." Ahosi stated.

Chapter 32

A myriad of chambers, unfathomable oceanic oors and interconnecting catacombs, a syndicate of powerful water spirits ate caviar from live sturgeons and drank re ned sperm whale with a touch of histidine. They looked alike, wore similar attire and resembled sinister, conniving jackals.

"Gentlemen to a good deed," Ehsraabmis toasted, his voice as husky as his body.

"We are closer and soon we will conquer, and walk the earth we shall." Tomuzi boastfully alluded.

"And roam the oceans and seas at will." Sivam conluded. A thunder of belly laughs, fins and legs thudding the floor ensued. Glittering and flickering of illuminant shades exposed skimpily dressed mermaids trapped in magical turves awaiting sultry.

Chapter 33

As the sun was about to go down on the fourth day, a rainbow appeared on the pothole. Kojo ran and sprinkled owers on top, signaling all is clear. Ama- nirenas grabbed his hand and sprang out with a knife around his neck. She was dressed in full armor as if she anticipated aggression.

"You have one chance, are you alone." Kojo hesitated. "No."

"You have broken your promise. You treacherous being, I cannot trust you, never come back." She sliced his cheek and jumped back into the pothole.

"It's about Vera." He yelled and stayed motionless, waiting for her reaction. She slowly emerged.

"How do you know that name?" She asked with a erce tone.

"I helped in her capture."

"You did what?"

"Sarais gave me the orders, he promised if I did it, I would be accepted among the water spirits."

"Do you know what you have just done?"

"No."

"Who is the mortal being, I saw in the sh's eye."

"His is a friend. His name is Chief Chirau."

"You brought a chief."

"He is a good chief."

"You know chiefs communicate with immortal beings

don't you."
He stammered. "Yes."
"Tell him to come out."
"Chief Chirau come out, everything is okay."
Chief Chirau stood up from behind the bushes and began to praise the ancestral spirits. "We are your children, I know that sometimes we disobey you, we go against your commands, we praise you and come to you for help, you are our elders, our leaders, we do whatever you ask us to do." Amanirenas was touched, something in her mind was triggered.
"Enough you are making me nervous." He walked over and stood in front of them.
Amanirenas still had the knife on Kojo's throat.
"He is only a boy, who wants to do what is right."
She laughed, "Only a boy, yes only a boy."
"The woman you are holding, we want her back." "Who do you think you are, you come here making demands. You want to die?
You are lucky you are our descendants."
"You abandoned us, we are slaves in our own land. Our children, your children are suffering. We have nothing to celebrate, yet we still worship you day and night."
Amanirenas softened and walked towards him. "Which ancestral line are you from chief."
Chief Chirau stood rmly, knowing he could be execu-ted at any moment.
"We are the great grandchildren of the Ngombe tribe, the great grandchildren of the Akongo the sup- reme being, father above all spirits. The lineage of the fearless and the gifted. The lion that eats other lions." She was almost in tears. Another voice distracted her. "Father of Mbokomu, the goddess of the Ngombe." In shock she

turned around and came face to face with Aragognot
Paradza. She gave a frantic cry, almost about to
crumble and she became invisible, running wildly
around the garden.

"We chose a different path, but we all come from one
being. The well being of our people is what we seek.
You might be an enemy, but we have a greater enemy
and soon our people will be wiped out from the face
of the earth. We come in peace. We are immortal, our
strength lies with the one above. The ancestors of the
woman you in imprisoned, her bloodline holds
the keys to our world. For us to defeat our enemies she
has to be sacri ced. The curse has to be reversed. Go
and tell the fearless goddess, we need her help."
There was a thud into the water and the ground closed.
"What have you done, the only person I ever loved has
gone. I will never see her again." Kojo sobbed.
There was an after shock, the enclave quaked and
began to disintegrate.

A silenced leader's gaze, stifles the oppressor.